Law and the Limits of Government

Law and the Limits of Government

Temporary versus Permanent Legislation

Frank Fagan

School of Law, Erasmus University Rotterdam, The Netherlands and Department of Economics, University of Bologna, Italy

Edward Elgar

Cheltenham, UK • Northampton, MA, USA

Published by
Edward Elgar Publishing Limited
The Lypiatts
15 Lansdown Road
Cheltenham
Glos GL50 2JA
UK

Edward Elgar Publishing, Inc.
William Pratt House
9 Dewey Court
Northampton
Massachusetts 01060
USA

A catalogue record for this book
is available from the British Library

Library of Congress Control Number: 2012954982

This book is available electronically in the ElgarOnline.com
Law Subject Collection, E-ISBN 978 0 85793 866 4

MIX
Paper from
responsible sources
FSC® C013056
FSC
www.fsc.org

ISBN 978 0 85793 865 7

Typeset by Servis Filmsetting Ltd, Stockport, Cheshire
Printed and bound in Great Britain by T.J. International Ltd, Padstow

Contents

Figures

Tables

Foreword

Francesco Parisi

In his book *Law and the Limits of Government: Temporary versus Permanent Legislation*, Frank Fagan addresses several important questions concerning the timing of legal intervention and duration of laws. These are questions that are central to any modern economic theory of lawmaking. These questions had been considered in the previous legal and economic literature. Fagan's book adds a novel voice in this area of law and economics, addressing these questions from a novel perspective with an intriguing mix of theoretical and empirical analysis. The theoretical analysis isolates three fundamental strategic relationships: (i) between legislators and citizens, (ii) between legislators and special interest groups, and (iii) between current legislators and future legislators. Each of these three dimensions of the legislative process hinges upon the timing and duration of legal intervention.

Unlike permanent legislation, temporary legislation governs for a limited time and has a default time of expiration. Fagan builds on the existing literature on norms and self-compliance to show that the effects of temporary legislation can outlive the legal effectiveness of temporary legislation. After its expiration, temporary legislation can continue to produce effects. Fagan further considers explanations for the fact that a large portion of legislation is permanent, notwithstanding the transactions-cost advantages of temporary legislation in the face of uncertainty. One such explanation comes from the legislator vs. special interest group relationship. According to Fagan, legislators lack full information to make laws. Industries and special interest groups often privately hold information. Interest groups may lack incentives to reveal such information, because revelation could run against their legislative interests. Legislators therefore use a threat of permanent legislation as a strategy to induce interest groups to reveal information that they would not otherwise reveal.

Temporary enactments may fail to signal a strong enough commitment from legislators, however, and might not induce disclosure of private information by interest groups.

Fagan's analysis of tax laws provides an explanation for a different pattern of legal intervention, that is, one based on the relationship between present and future lawmakers. According to Fagan, on issues dealing with fiscal and financial policy we are likely to observe a more frequent use of temporary legislation. The reason is that by passing a temporary fiscal law today, current legislatures force future lawmakers to incur political costs by voting on an extension at a later date. By adopting temporary legislation, current lawmakers externalize political costs onto future lawmakers.

In this book, Fagan develops a multi-faceted theory showing under which conditions lawmakers might employ one or the other lawmaking strategy. The theory is tested with interesting empirical evidence. Using data taken from the 110th American Congress, Fagan shows that temporary legislation is more likely to become law than permanent legislation. Yet the magnitude of that likelihood varies across legislative committees. The variance, according to Fagan, demonstrates that the choice of temporary or permanent legislation is optimized around the pattern of legal intervention and its relevant strategic relationship.

The data is further employed to show that in some policy domains, older legislative sponsors prefer permanent legislation to temporary legislation, even in the face of higher transactions-cost. Fagan suggests that the evidence reflects the desire of older legislators to leave statutory legacies. Conversely, the data shows that younger legislative sponsors prefer temporary legislation to permanent legislation. Because temporary legislation is more likely to become law, that preference may reflect the desire of younger legislators to sponsor a greater number of passed laws generally, so that they might develop their careers and project competence to interest groups in future elections.

Despite its catchy title, *Law and the Limits of Government: Temporary versus Permanent Legislation* is not a good pick for casual or bedtime reading. Notwithstanding the general relevance of the topic, it is a dense and purely academic book. Its findings, however, illuminate the reality of political rulemaking and will hopefully stimulate a different popular understanding of the peculiar patterns of lawmaking observed in modern legislatures.

Acknowledgements

I thank the publishers and copyright holders listed here for their permission to reprint the excerpts indicated.

Fagan, Frank, After the sunset: The residual effect of temporary legislation. *European Journal of Law and Economics*. Copyright © 2011 Springer Publishing Company, Frank Fagan. Reprinted with permission.

Fagan, Frank and Faure, Michael, Response: The role of lawmakers, lobbyists, and interest groups in the normative evaluation of timing rules. 160 *University of Pennsylvania Law Review*, *PENNumbra* 61 (2011). Copyright © 2011 Frank Fagan, Michael Faure. Reprinted with permission.

I also thank the European Commission, and its support of the European Doctorate in Law and Economics, through which a portion of this work benefitted. Lastly, I thank the scholars who helped shape this book: Firat Bilgel for his discussions on temporary legislation and his specific contribution to the empirical analysis of chapter 6; David Herring for his discussions on temporary tax legislation and his guidance with respect to the development of chapter 5; Urmee Khan for her contribution to the theoretical model developed in chapter 2; and especially Michael Faure, Luigi Franzoni, and Francesco Parisi for providing general guidance and criticism throughout the development of the ideas contained within this book.

PART I

Theory

1. Introduction

Legislatures are inherently limited. Apart from the difficulties posed by collective choice that judicial and administrative lawmaking can largely circumvent, legislatures face additional difficulties adjusting their laws when adjustment is needed or desired. At the very least, repeals or amendments must be placed on the legislative agenda and thus face opportunity cost comparisons across other legislative actions. Unfavorable cost comparisons can slow or indefinitely suspend legislative adjustment. Meanwhile the initial enactment will continue to govern. To the contrary, when legislation is passed temporarily, it can provide more substantive flexibility than permanent legislation. Precise rules need not be codified to govern for an indefinite duration by default, and can instead be adjusted periodically. Moreover, temporary legislation forces itself onto the legislative agenda at expiration; the legislature must decide to extend the provision in its current form, extend it in a different form, or let it expire completely.

Early law and economics studies that addressed the optimal levels of statutory and judge-made law such as Ehrlich and Posner (1974) were not so much interested in normatively prescribing one type of law over the other. They were more interested in specifying a set of conditions where one type of law would simply perform better. Thus they concluded that statutory law should be favored when legal precision is greatly valued, and that judge-made law should be favored when legal flexibility is greatly valued.

The analysis contained in this book is related to that work in both content and approach. In content, permanent legislation is similar to the statutory law of Ehrlich and Posner (1974); temporary legislation is its more flexible alternative. In approach, this book is less interested in advocating greater use of temporary or permanent legislation at the expense of the other, and is more interested in specifying the sets of conditions where one type of legislation will simply perform better with respect to social welfare maximization.

Law and economics first examined temporary legislation in the early 1980s, a time in which sunsets were being pushed by American advocacy groups in an effort to limit the size of the central governments of the late 1970s. Judge Calabresi, in a book entitled *A Common Law for the Age of Statutes* (1982), was critical of the sunset movement, and perhaps rightly so, since sunsets failed to reduce the size of government as intended. Most were simply rubber-stamped by the legislature for extension as soon as they expired. Accordingly, the prevailing view within law and economics continued to deduce that legislative lawmaking, temporary or not, promoted entrenchment of legal rules and reduced legal flexibility. The prevailing view would eventually associate legislative lawmaking with slow economic growth (La Portal et al., 2008).

As the use of sunsets for legislative oversight began to wane, the scholarship began to pay less and less attention to what it understood as a short-lived (and ill-advised) government accountability movement. Then in the early 2000s, the American legislature began passing tax cuts and credits temporarily, and no longer were sunsets simply rubber-stamped. The scholarship responded theoretically with Garrett (2004) and Kysar (2006) criticizing the practice, and Yin (2009) supporting it. Public-economics scholarship weighed in as well, detailing the optimal length of the budget window for avoiding the socially suboptimal use of sunsets (Auerbach 2006, Dharmapala 2006).

Also amid controversy, normatively charged legislation such as the Violent Crime Control and Law Enforcement Act of 1994 (gun control) and portions of the USA PATRIOT Act of 2001 (domestic surveillance) were passed temporarily as a way to reduce opposition. By the mid-2000s, it was clear that the contemporary use of temporary legislation was being pushed beyond legislative oversight and into areas rich with strategic considerations between political parties, as seen in taxation, and between the legislature and citizens, as seen in socially controversial policy domains.

Yet a further strategic interaction can be induced with temporary legislation between the legislature and a special interest group. Gersen (2007) provided a case study of the temporary passage of the Terrorism Risk Insurance Act of 2002 to illustrate, and chapter 4 models this interaction referencing that case study throughout. Gersen (2007) is of special note as it is the first systematic and contemporary examination of temporary legislation. The article demonstrates with considerable detail that temporary legislation has a historical pedigree that stretches back at least to the American founding era. Further, its use then bears resemblance to its use now. With respect to taxation, the American constitution limited all appropriations for raising and supporting armies to a term no longer than two years. Trade with Indian tribes was regulated temporarily as well, and likely involved organized interests similar to those of a modern special interest group. Gersen (2007) documents a continued usage of temporary legislation well into the nineteenth and twentieth centuries. The sustained attention that temporary legislation has finally received today seems well deserved.

In addition to the literature specific to temporary legislation, Gersen and Posner (2007) and Luppi and Parisi (2009) have examined the family of legislative tools to which temporary legislation belongs. Temporary legislation is one of several other types of timing rules that permit legislators to specify the actual days that a statute will be in effect. There are delay timing rules, which allow a statute to be enacted today but come into force at a later date. There are deferment, anticipatory, and conditional timing rules under which a statute might be enacted but come into force only if certain specified conditions are met. Each type of timing rule has its own set of strategic considerations, and the theoretical literature is growing.

The principal inquiry of this book is what role the choice of temporary legislation plays in the maximization of social welfare. We begin by examining the choice of temporary versus permanent legislation when law leaves residual effects. We introduce the concept of residual effects in order to aggregate the various theories that purport that law influences behavior independently of its continued codification. For example, law can be expressive, and thereby change existing levels of social sanctioning. If the law is repealed or expires, sanctioning levels may continue to be influenced by the previous legal environment. Similarly, law can inform or create focal points that change organizational or coordinative behavior. Again, if repealed or expired, the behavior may continue to be influenced by the previous legal environment. Other examples include temporary protective tariffs that leave behind new markets or consumer tastes, and lobbies or coalitions that form around a temporary legislative agenda, only to remain intact to pursue other policies once the temporary legislation expires.

In chapter 2 we focus on the residual compliance effect of temporary legislation, and find that it can decrease total legislation costs. Because temporary legislation can, for example, change the state of social norms and lead to increased compliance, legislators can minimize legislation costs with a series of temporary enactments. At each moment of reenactment, passage is less costly since the law has had some time to change the state of social norms and induce further compliance independent of formal enforcement. In controversial policy domains, temporary legislation may be easier to enact in its future instances because it has had time to update social sanctioning levels throughout a population. In addition, the temporary nature of the legislation makes the law easier to pass at its initial stage because the public perceives it to last for a shorter length of time than permanent legislation. Both of these reasons help explain the use of temporary timing rules for controversial policies such as gun control and domestic surveillance. Chapter 2 examines and compares the compliance effects of temporary and permanent legislation in the short to medium term, and specifies the conditions for each legislative type to maximize social welfare.

Even when the choice of temporary legislation may be socially efficient from a short- to medium-term transactions cost perspective, legislators may still prefer permanent legislation. While permanent legislation may offer larger material benefits to legislators, an important reason why legislators may prefer higher cost permanent legislation is that they may be interested in leaving a legacy of statutory rules or normative influence that extends beyond their careers. Chapter 3 examines this possibility, paying special attention to legislators' ability to generate long-term normative influence. The chapter models the creation of long-term normative influence dynamically, where at its extreme endpoint, a person involuntarily complies absent formal enforcement such as fines or incarceration, or informal enforcement such as pride, guilt, approval, or disapproval. It is likely that the legislator has a less ambitious compliance effect in mind while choosing to legislate permanently, and the model thus explains various degrees of normative legacy for the legislator, including those less impactful than involuntary compliance. Importantly, the model emphasizes that legislators can create and foster an expressive effect of law directly. Contemporary law and economics has largely attributed the expressive effect (i.e. norm creation and updates in social sanctioning levels) to the law itself, or broadly to the state. In some cases, however, legislators play a very direct role in creating or changing normative behavior. The model emphasizes that role.

Taken together, chapters 2 and 3 provide the theoretical analysis of the strategic interaction between legislators and citizens. Chapter 4 turns to the strategic interaction between legislators and a special interest group. Sometimes a special interest group possesses information that legislators desire for lawmaking. This was the circumstance surrounding the Terrorism Risk Insurance Act of 2002 detailed in Gersen (2007). While special interest groups will not reveal that information if it is not in their interest to do so, legislators may induce revelation with new legislation. Chapter 4 examines the conditions under which a special interest group will reveal in spite of the fact that the legislation is enacted temporarily. In some cases, a special interest group will not reveal and simply wait for the legislation to expire, but in others, temporary legislation can induce revelation, especially when the special interest group receives reputation benefits from revealing. It normatively follows that legislators should increase reputation benefits to special interest groups when legislator and special interest group interests are unaligned, as long as the cost structure of temporary legislation is superior to the cost structure of permanent legislation. Chapter 4 presents an additional finding. Generally, most of the current literature on timing rules supposes that temporary legislation introduces uncertainty and curtails private investment. To the contrary, chapter 4 provides the conditions for which temporary legislation can introduce certainty. Generally, when the legislature is pursuing a policy objective, a temporary timing rule can demonstrate that the legislature is serious about getting the policy right, and therefore signals the certainty of a particular legal environment regardless of the temporary status of the governing legislation.

The final chapter of Part I takes up a special case of temporary legislation, viz. temporary taxation. Temporary taxation highlights the use of temporary legislation to facilitate a strategic interaction between a current legislature and a future legislature. While most of the literature on temporary taxation has condemned its use because it increases rent extraction and introduces uncertainty for private investors, our analysis demonstrates that both of those reasons are normatively ambiguous with respect to social welfare. Nonetheless temporary taxation is socially inefficient because legislators use temporary taxation as a reelection strategy, and in the process, externalize political costs onto their opponents and social costs of debt service onto the public. The public finance literature, namely Auerbach (2006), suggests that the length of the budget window should be set so as to minimize the strategic use of sunsets. However, that study fails to adequately account for the routine circumvention of budgetary offset requirements by the American legislature. Because of circumvention, legislators will continue to externalize costs at any length of the budget window. Our normative prescription therefore involves constitutionally stipulating that temporary tax cuts or spending increases and their offsets take immediate effect.

Part II addresses the theory contained in Part I with empirical study using data from the 110th American Congress (2007–09). Chapter 6 compares the probabilities that temporary or permanent legislation become law. It also compares those probabilities within a variety of policy domains that are assumed to vary in their ability to generate residual effects. The analysis finds that temporary legislation more easily becomes law in general, and that the probability exhibits variance across policy domains. For example, temporary bills that originate in the Judiciary committee are more likely to become law than temporary bills that originate in the Veterans Affairs committee. This suggests that certain policy domains are more favorable for temporary legislation than others, perhaps according to their capability to generate cost-reducing residual effects, and provides support for the theory set out in chapter 2. It should be noted that because no two bills are substantively alike, we compare the average passage probability of temporary bills with the average passage probability of permanent bills. Because of the limitation, there is a possibility that our data does not perfectly account for the fact that substantive provisions can drive passage probability, as can temporal restrictions. Nonetheless, the model helps formalize the intuition found in the existing literature, i.e., that temporary legislation passes more easily. In addition, the interaction between substance and temporal restrictions is somewhat mitigated by controlling for the bill's committee of origin.

Chapter 7 tests whether or not the age of the legislation's sponsor explains the choice of a temporary versus permanent timing rule. Chapter 3 purports that older legislators value leaving a statutory legacy or normative influence to future generations more so than younger legislators. Thus older legislators are more likely to sponsor permanent legislation than temporary legislation. The study finds moderate support for this theory, and offers some qualified evidence.

In sum, the book examines the choice of temporary versus permanent legislation within three strategic settings. Chapters 2 and 3 examine the interaction between legislators and citizens, chapter 4 between legislators and a lobby, and chapter 5 between current legislators and future legislators. The empirical chapters 6 and 7 primarily focus on the interaction between legislators and citizens, though they do present implications relevant for the relationship between legislators and interest groups that are narrower than the general citizenry.

2. Short- to medium-term residual effects

2.1 INTRODUCTION

Legislatures can pass legislation temporarily by including a duration or "sunset" clause that automatically invalidates a statute on a specified date. These clauses allow the legislature to authorize a statute for a limited time and govern temporarily. In contrast to "normal" permanent legislation, temporary legislation does not require additional legislative action for its rescission. It loses any legally binding effect when it reaches its predetermined date of expiration and can only be extended if the legislature passes a new bill that specifies an additional period of legal validity. Recent literature on legislative timing rules treats the effect of temporary legislation as dependent upon the continued existence of a legally binding rule (Parisi et al. 2004, Gersen 2007, Gersen and Posner 2007, Luppi and Parisi 2009, Yin 2009). The discussion assumes that when legislation expires, any compliance effect associated with that legislation also expires. No explicit consideration is given to the possibility that legislation can produce effects independent of statutory enforcement. For example, temporary law can be expressive, and change the level of social sanctioning around the substance of a law (Cooter 1998, McAdams and Rasmusen 2005, Funk 2007, Feldman 2009). Temporary industry regulations can lead to the permanent destruction of an industry or the emergence of substitute products (Nye 2007). Lobbies and coalitions can form around temporary policies, and can remain in place to seek other opportunities after a temporary policy expires (Rasmusen 1993, Grossman and Helpman 2001). Temporary policies that inform or create focal points can permanently change modes of coordination (Dharmapala and McAdams 2003). Generally, policies that change prevailing behavior can leave residual effects, even after those policies have expired.

This chapter extends the research on timing rules by examining the interrelation between the choice of temporary timing rule and its post-expiration effect. When temporary laws leave residual effects, the benefits of lawmaking that the literature has confined to the period of statutory enforcement can spill over into future periods, where statutory enforcement is no longer in place. If legislators can anticipate such a spillover, then they may choose a temporary timing rule instead of a permanent timing rule to save costs, or to carry out other strategic concerns. This chapter explicitly deals with how legislators can choose timing rules to save costs.

Residual expressive effects

The model accounts for any type of residual effect upon expiration of a temporary law. However, the case of residual expressive effects deserves further preliminary explanation. Whether or not a law can create residual expressive effects in the first place depends on whether or not a law is expressive. Expressive theory posits that in the absence of any formal enforcement such as imprisonment or fines, legislatures can affect informal enforcement such as guilt, pride, disapproval, or approval through new legislation. The legislature induces informal enforcement through the expression of its opinion, much like a norm entrepreneur, by passing new legislation that is substantively normative. People who have already internalized an "obedience to law" norm will feel new guilt or pride when disobeying or obeying the substance of new legislation (Cooter 2000). On the other hand, the new legislation may increase the willingness of people to normatively sanction or reward others with disapproval or approval (Cooter 1998).[1]

Later research in expressive law contends that respect for the legal system and willingness to judge others comes from a strong alignment between state and citizen preferences, and a strong alignment between the state's sense of fairness with the citizen's intuitive sense of fairness. For the purpose of this chapter, we only note that when new legislation is expressive it can create new levels of guilt, pride, disapproval and approval throughout the citizenry. In our model, the magnitudes of those new levels can range from marginal

---

[1] New laws can also induce informal enforcement by signaling what others disapprove of or approve of, thereby changing the expected cost of an infraction (McAdams 2000b).

additions to broad cascades such as those described in Bikhchandani et al. (1992) and Sunstein (1996). We will refer generally to these processes in the model as updates in normative relations, which can lead to increases in the desirability of expressive legislation. Of import for lawmakers, is that after an update, the cost of future reauthorizations of temporary legislation can decrease.[2]

To the extent that lawmakers expect a decrease in reauthorization costs from legal expression, the costs of passing temporary or permanent legislation up front should converge and the possibility for the legislator to save on costs should approach zero. For if an enactment changes normative relations and is expected to reduce the costs of a future reauthorization, that future cost reduction would be reflected in a higher cost initial enactment in equilibrium. In other words, the demand side must pay for the ability to change normative relations and to lower future legislation costs. On the other hand, as the supply side includes voters, that future reduction in costs can only be perfectly reflected in an enactment cost if voters are consciously "selling" changes in their normative relations. In a time-consistent equilibrium, voters do not update their normative relations until the law is enacted. For this reason, we assume that voters are not selling those changes up front, but to some extent permitting the law to be "costlessly" expressive over time in exchange for utility derived from pride and approval. Under this assumption, future reauthorizations would price inefficiently, and a reauthorization of temporary legislation should therefore pass more easily.

In the dynamic setting, where temporary laws update normative relations and induce normative compliance outcomes (independent of the continued existence of legally binding rules), it becomes possible that timing rules may be chosen by the legislature for reasons other than what the literature has demonstrated thus far. In addition to providing regulatory flexibility in an uncertain legal environment, timing rules may be chosen for their ability to dynamically mitigate the high costs of legislating in policy domains that are normatively contestable. Many policies that face high levels of opposition such as

---

2 There is a growing literature that demonstrates the opposite effect, where new legal expression crowds out existing informal enforcement. For example, Depoorter and Vanneste (2006) gives evidence that expressive copyright law leads to increases in copyright infringement. In our context, future temporary extension costs would increase.

domestic surveillance, gun control, and taxation frequently employ temporary provisions.[3] While temporary provisions can make those laws easier to pass in their first instance, our model demonstrates that a temporary expressive effect can make those laws easier to pass in the future.

2.2 THE MODEL

The model describes a unit measure of agents, with heterogeneous preferences independently drawn from an absolutely continuous distribution. Legislators minimize costs based upon their anticipation of the post-expiration effect of legislation.[4] We refer to the post-expiration effect generally as compliance for exposition.[5]

The model has a two-period time-line. At the beginning of the game, the true state of the world is unknown, i.e. the actual effectiveness of the chosen policy in producing compliance is unknown. In period 1, the legislators move first to choose $\tau \in \{0, 1\}$, the binary decision between a temporary timing rule (0) and a permanent timing rule (1). Agents then set their intra- and interagent relations and choose their compliance levels. In period 2, legislators decide either to reauthorize the temporary legislation or let it expire, or to repeal the permanent legislation or let it continue. In our formal model, period 2 is notional. Its significance is that at the beginning of the period, legislators can observe a signal related to the true state, i.e. they become better aware of the effectiveness of the policy in producing compliance. The precision of that signal is assumed

3 USA PATRIOT Act, Pub. L. No. 107-56, 115 Stat. 272, 285 (2001). Section 110105 of the Violent Crime Control and Law Enforcement Act of 1994; Pub. L. No. 103-322, 108 Stat. 1796 (1994), codified at 18 USC § 1033 et seq (2000). On taxation, see chapter 5.

4 Thus the model follows the existing literature on timing rules by examining the behavior of a majority group of legislators with heterogeneous preferences. Posner and Vermeule (2008) give several recent scenarios from the 107th and 110th Congresses. For a different approach, where timing rules are the outcome of gridlock within the legislature, see Auerbach (2006).

5 Our use of compliance underscores that temporary lawmaking goals can continue to be realized after sunset. However, any post-expiration behavioral or organizational change may be conceived without affecting our results.

to be increasing in the level of compliance chosen by the agents in period 1.[6]

Contingent on the assumption that signal precision is increasing in the level of compliance, it is reasonable to assume that a more precise signal will lead to a better decision. Hence the underlying premise of the model is that the value of a period 2 decision by legislators is increasing, for both the legislators and the agents, in the period 1 level of compliance by agents. We capture this aspect by introducing a "value of revealed information" term in the objective functions of the players. By backward induction, in any equilibrium, legislators will take into account the agents' best response and choose τ accordingly in period 1. The order of play can be summarized as:

1. Legislators choose the timing rule, τ, from set $\{0,1\}$, where (0) is a temporary timing rule and (1) is a permanent timing rule.
2. Agents are matched within period 1 to play a game where they set their intra- and interagent relations.
3. At the end of that period, agents choose their compliance levels.
4. Legislators observe the aggregate compliance level and decide either to reauthorize the temporary legislation or let it expire, or to repeal the permanent legislation or let it continue.

In the following section, we demonstrate how agents set their relations when legislators impose new legislation. The state of agent relations that prevails determines how agents choose their optimal compliance level, shown in section 2.2. Lastly in section 2.3, we show that by backward induction, legislators will take into account the agents' best response compliance level and choose to legislate temporarily or permanently.

2.2.1 Agent Relations

Before agents choose their compliance levels, agents first set their intra- and interagent relations in response to new legislation which yields population state γ. The introduction of γ allows us to account for how the prevailing state of behavior throughout the population

---

[6] This assumption rests on the reasoning that the higher the compliance level, the more visible is the policy outcome.

affects the agents' choice of compliance. Thus, any payoff from compliance is dependent upon not only contemporary statutory enforcement, but upon any previous change in cost structure from past statutory enforcement in addition.

For example, a person may experience a change in their intrapersonal relations when the legislature passes a new law. One who has internalized an obedience to law norm permits the new law to change the magnitudes of their guilt cost for noncompliance or of their pride benefit from compliance. The fact that the behavior is now legally sanctioned produces new magnitudes. There can be preexisting levels of guilt and pride for the behavior embodied in the law, but upon being codified, those levels are increased if legislation is expressive. If the legislation is not expressive, then those levels remain unaffected (Cooter 2000). Similarly, a person can permit a new law to update their interpersonal relations which govern their willingness to disapprove or approve of another person's noncompliance or compliance. The fact that the behavior is now codified makes a person more willing to sanction others if the legislation is expressive. If it is not, their willingness remains at preexisting levels (Cooter 1998). While statutory enforcement may impact the cost of compliance, the law may additionally induce a change in the cost of compliance through its impact upon the constellation of intra- and interagent relations. A change in normative relations changes the cost structure of compliance, and the expiration of a temporary policy does not necessarily return those normative relations to their pre-policy levels.

In the case of temporary policies that inform, agent relations are updated when a person becomes aware of a new policy either through direct communication from lawmakers, or through interagent learning. Once the temporary policy expires, agents may retain coordinative information that continues to affect their choice of compliance. Or in the case of temporary tariffs or regulations, firms update their behavior when they expect the benefits of adapting to a temporary policy to outweigh the costs of waiting for the policy to potentially expire. Here, an update in behavior can continue to administer a regulatory effect after the sunset. For example, the firm may have incurred costs that restrain entry or exit through the adoption of a new production process or through other adaptations to the temporary legal environment. If the firm does not incur those costs and chooses to wait for the temporary policy to expire instead, we understand that no update has taken place.

In the case of resource allocation toward creating policies, the lobbies and coalitions that are updated or formed to create temporary policies may continue to seek other legislative or regulatory opportunities once a temporary policy has expired. If an existing lobby or coalition creates the new policy, or if the new lobby or coalition has no effect beyond the temporary policy, again we understand that no update has taken place. Generally, after the legislature passes a law the agent chooses $m \in \{U, -U\}$, where (U) denotes the decision to update some composite measure of their intra- and interagent relations and ($-U$) denotes the decision to not update.

Strategic agent relations

The agent relations game below maps the interaction between two agents after the legislature has passed a new law, and after each agent has chosen to update or not update. Each of the players has private knowledge regarding whether or not the new law has been caused by an internal update. That knowledge is revealed when player 1 complies or does not comply with the behavior embodied in the new law when in the presence of the other agent. If she complies, player 1 reveals that she has updated her agent relations, always intrapersonally since she moves first in time with no knowledge of player 2's potential sanction by construction. Upon observing player 1's behavior, player 2 chooses to sanction or to not sanction player 1. If player 2 sanctions player 1, player 2 reveals that she has updated her interagent relations. Otherwise, she reveals that no interagent update has taken place.[7]

We examine the case where $((a - c)(d - b)) < 0$ and the game (Γ) has a single dominant strategy equilibrium, and where ($a > c$, $d > b$) and the game is a problem of coordination. An aspiration and imitation model is used to examine repeated play.[8]

---

[7] For knowledge to be revealed to both players, it is necessary that the players interact. What the players observe or do not observe in each other reveals information. Zasu (2008) constructs a model that shows that higher levels of interaction, or connectivity within groups, can result in higher levels of sanctioning.

[8] Aspiration and imitation models are based upon processes where agents compare their actual payoff to an aspired payoff, and as a result of that comparison, sometimes choose a different strategy by imitating others. They are often employed for modeling the emergence of social norms. See

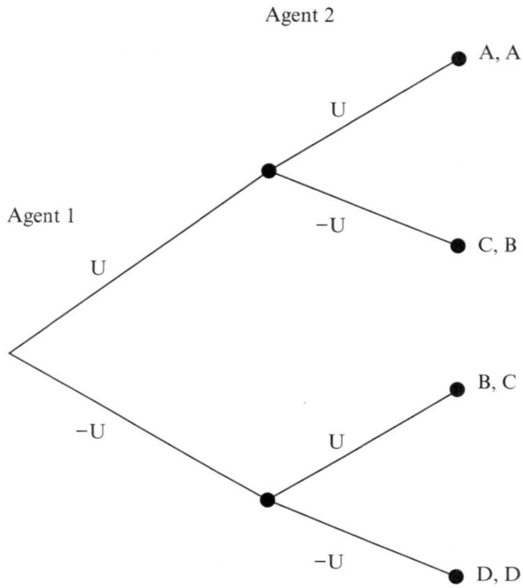

Figure 2.1 A stylized model of agent relations

Dynamic agent relations

When player 1 is not sanctioned or player 2 observes noncompliance, they learn that one other agent has not permitted the new law to change their behavior. On the other hand, when player 1 is sanctioned or player 2 observes compliance, they learn that one other agent has permitted the new law to change their behavior. What they learn gives their actual payoff, ranging from the value of incurring no costs or receiving no benefits to the value of incurring some costs or receiving some benefits. Costs might reflect industry sanctioning from following or not following a temporary policy, especially when concerted action may lead to a temporary extension or expiration of a regulation (Coglianese et al. (2004)). Benefits might reflect increased profits and enhanced government relations. In other contexts, costs may take the form of sanctioning from competitor lobbies or lost coalition opportunities, and benefits may take the form of rents extracted from legislative and regulatory

---

Binmore and Samuelson (1997), Samuelson, L. (1997), Benaim and Weibull (2003), Traulsen et al. (2005).

opportunities. In the case of a temporary policy that is expressive, the costs of noncompliance may be understood as internal guilt and external disapproval from fellow citizens. The benefits of compliance may be understood as pride and approval.

Generally, the payoff from updating or not updating is interdependent. This actual payoff that agents learn from interacting with other agents is then compared to an aspired level of what the agent thinks is appropriate.[9] If the actual payoff deviates from an aspired payoff, players may be motivated to choose to update or to not update by imitating their previous opponent in the next iteration of the game. For this reason, we are particularly interested in examining the cases where the levels of A, B, C and D result in each coordination profile (U, U) and $(-U, -U)$ as Nash equilibria.[10]

Consider the symmetric 2×2 game given in Figure 2.1 where there is a single finite population of N agents. Let time be discretely divided into intervals of length t. During each iteration, an agent is characterized by their pure strategy (U) or $(-U)$ that she implements in that iteration. During each iteration of length t, pairs of agents are randomly drawn to play one game. They are drawn independently and without replacement, and the various ways that they can be matched are equally probable. Their payoffs A, B, C and D are expected. Actual realized payoffs are random, given by the expected payoff of A, B, C or D plus the outcome R of a random variable $\widetilde{R}$. This variable has an expected value of 0. It is included to capture any random shock that disturbs the player's payoffs, and is intended to

---

[9] The aspired level can be based upon their prior levels of guilt, pride, disapproval, and approval before interacting. Other likely bases for aspiration levels include higher-order expectations such as what an agent thinks some outside authority thinks the payoff should be (Lewis 1969). For our results to hold, it is sufficient to assume that only some type of comparison is taking place.

[10] In the context of new expressive laws or industry regulations particularly, it may be that the strategy distribution is relatively unknown until a sufficient level of interaction has taken place. What one learns from interaction, namely the other person's strategy to update or to not update, can serve as a metric for the general level of receptivity to the new law throughout the community. Moreover, since coordination around updating or not updating leads to higher levels of guilt, pride, disapproval, and approval, imitation profiles (U, U) and $(-U, -U)$ are likely to emerge.

highlight any complication that the players may encounter in identifying their payoffs precisely, apart from simply choosing between (U) and $(-U)$.[11]

When an agent plays update and meets another agent who plays update, her expected payoff is A and her realized payoff is $A + R$. If she updates her agent relations in a population where a proportion k is also updating, then her expected payoff is given by

$$\pi_U(k) = kA + (1 - k)C \tag{2.1}$$

where her expectation is taken with respect to both the likely identity of her opponent and the likely realization of $\tilde{R}$. If she chooses to not update in a population where a proportion k is updating, then her expected payoff $\pi_{-U}(k)$ is given by

$$\pi_{-U}(k) = kB + (1 - k)D \tag{2.2}$$

During each iteration t, each person draws from an independently distributed Bernoulli random variable. Let the time units of measure be chosen so that with probability t, the distribution yields the outcome learn. With the probability $1 - t$, the distribution yields the outcome not learn. A person who receives a learn draw remembers her realized payoff of the previous iteration and evaluates it as satisfactory or unsatisfactory. If her realized payoff exceeds her aspiration level, then she evaluates her strategy as satisfactory and maintains that strategy in the following iteration of the game. If her realized payoff does not exceed her aspiration level, she loses confidence in her current strategy and abandons it. When, for example, a person plays update in a population in which everyone plays update, and then receives a learn draw, the corresponding probability that she abandons the update strategy is

$$g(A) = prob(A + R < \Delta) = F(\Delta - A) \tag{2.3}$$

---

[11] While Fudenberg and Harris (1992) build a model where $\tilde{R}$ is correlated across agents, that is, where environmental factors impose a common risk to all agents, we treat the distribution of $\tilde{R}$ as independently and identically distributed. In this case its distribution does not depend on the selection of strategy.

where Δ is her aspiration level, R is the realization of random payoff variable $\tilde{R}$, and F is the cumulative distribution of $\tilde{R}$. Similar expressions can be given for payoffs B, C and D.

Following Samuelson, L. (1997), we assume F is uniform along the interval $[-\omega, \omega]$, where payoffs $\{A, B, C, D\} \subset [\Delta - \omega, \Delta + \omega]$.[12] The Uniform distribution's linearity permits the passing of a player's expectations through function g given by equation 2.3. Hence, when a person plays update and a proportion of the population playing update is k, then the probability that she abandons update is given by

$$g(\pi_U(k)) = F(\Delta - \pi_U(k)) \tag{2.4}$$

If agent i evaluates her payoff as unsatisfactory and abandons it in the next iteration of the game, she must now choose a strategy. We assume that she randomly selects another member j from the population. With probability $1 - \lambda$, she imitates j's strategy.[13] With probability λ, agent i chooses to not imitate j. In this case, she is a "mutant" or "asocial," and chooses to play the opposite strategy of j.

Within this framework, various relational outcomes can be imagined. For example, upon learning of a new law, a person may not have developed a new source of guilt for noncompliant behavior. Thus she does not experience a normative update. Suppose she comes into contact with another person who has experienced a normative update. She approaches the interaction with an aspiration payoff in mind, justified in part by her own level of guilt (in this case it can be 0). If her payoff is unsatisfactory because, for example, the other person disapproved of her noncompliance and made her feel guilt, she may abandon her strategy to not update her normative relations. Given a learn draw, she may instead choose to imitate j (i.e. update her normative relations) with probability $1 - \lambda$, leading to compliance or noncompliance independent of her initial reaction to an expressive law.

---

12 The Uniform distribution satisfies the monotone likelihood ratio property, which is necessary and sufficient for it to be more likely that low average expected payoffs produce low average realized payoffs. This condition allows realized payoffs to provide a useful basis for strategy evaluation.

13 It is possible that she may play the same strategy that she played in the game's first iteration, after receiving confirmation from j that update or not update may in fact be the best reply.

Infinite population

Let $\hat{\gamma}$ be a replicator of the form

$$\hat{\gamma} = \gamma(\pi_U(\gamma) + \lambda(1 - 2\gamma)(K - \bar{\pi})) \tag{2.5}$$

where $\gamma \in [0, 1]$ is the fraction of an infinite population playing update, $\bar{\pi} = \gamma\pi_U(\gamma) + (1 - \gamma)\pi_{-U}(\gamma)$ is the expected payoff, K is a constant which does not depend on the prevailing state of agent relations, and where

$$\pi_U(\gamma) = \gamma A + (1 - \gamma)C \tag{2.6}$$

$$\pi_{-U}(\gamma) = \gamma B + (1 - \gamma)D \tag{2.7}$$

These two equations are similar to equations 2.1–2.2 in that they replace k with γ. $\pi_U(\gamma)$ gives the expected payoff to an agent playing update when the proportion γ of her opponents play update. If a finite population were at state γ, meaning that proportion γ of the population were playing update, then a person playing update faces a population that also plays update in a slightly smaller proportion γ. As the population reaches infinity, this distinction disappears and γ becomes both the proportion playing update and the current state of agent relations.

For a population of size N and a time period length t, the aspiration and imitation model is a Markov process with $N + 1$ population states $u \in \{0, v, 2v, \ldots, 1\}$, where $v = 1/N$ and uN is the number of agents playing update in state u. By examining the double limit as N gets large and t gets small, we allow the aspiration and imitation model to be governed by the replicator given in equation 2.5. Now, instead of state $u\,(t)$ describing the number of agents playing update at moment t defined on discrete points $\{0, t, 2t, \ldots\}$, state $\gamma\,(t)$ describes a deterministic solution to the differential equation γ, which takes on values in [0, 1]. This permits the probabilities from moving one step to the right or left to be calculated for a given state u, which in turn can be used to construct an approximation of the behavior of the agent relations game over time.[14]

---

[14] By focusing on short time periods, the probability that two persons receive the learn draw, potentially moving u by more than one step, is negligible.

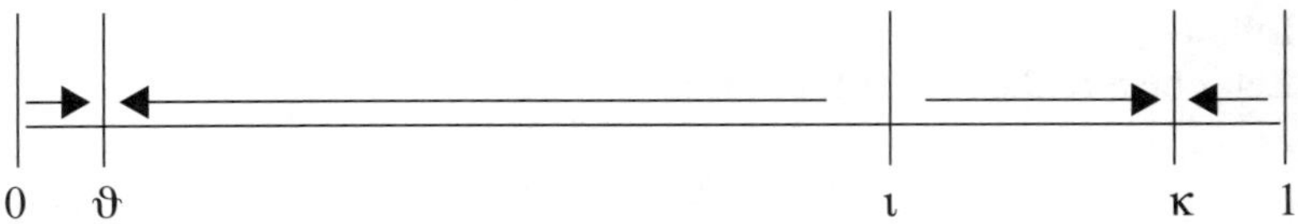

Figure 2.2 Phase diagram for the agent relations game with replicator dynamics

Suppose $\gamma(t)$ is governed by the replicator given in equation 2.5 with the boundary condition that $\gamma(0) = u(0)$. When Γ is a coordination game such that $(a > c, d > b)$, there are three Nash equilibria, two in pure strategies given by (U, U) and $(-U, -U)$, and one in mixed strategies. Three stationary states ϑ, ι, and κ exist, satisfying $0<\vartheta<\iota<\kappa<1$ (Samuelson, L. 1997, Proposition 3.1). The inner stationary state ι is unstable, but ϑ and κ are asymptotically stable with attraction basins $[0, \iota)$ and $(\iota, 1]$. As $\lambda \rightarrow 0$, each of the stationary states converge to the three Nash equilibria of Γ. Stationary state ϑ converges to the equilibrium where all agents play (U). Stationary state κ converges to the equilibrium where all agents play $(-U)$. Stationary state ι converges to the mixed equilibrium.

Suppose the legislator observes a stationary state of agent relations $\gamma(0) = u(0)$ within the basin $[0, \iota)$. The replicator will move close to ϑ where the agents are playing the profile (U,U), and remain in its vicinity forever. Similarly, when the legislator observes state $\gamma(0) = u(0)$ within the basin $(\iota, 1]$, the replicator will move close to κ where the agents are playing the profile $(-U,-U)$, and remain in its vicinity forever.

When payoffs are such that strategies (U) or $(-U)$ dominate, we will see that lawmakers can more easily evaluate period 2 legislation costs. On the other hand, we would have to impose very strong informational assumptions for players to be able to clearly identify dominant strategies in the agent relations game that are procedurally time consistent. Agents are likely to remain ignorant of the strategy distribution throughout the population until some level of interaction with other agents occurs. Moreover, when agent relations are characterized by coordination, it is likely that no strategy yet dominates and multiple equilibria still exist. Although period 2 legislation costs are more ambiguous in this scenario, legislators may still be able to optimize on timing rule selection. If legislators observe a stationary state within either coordination basin, the replicator dynamics will move close to ϑ or κ and remain in either vicinity forever. We only need to suppose that players reject strategies that yield payoffs that fall short of an aspired level, and instead imitate.

2.2.2 Agent's Optimal Compliance

Once agents set their relations, they choose their optimal compliance level for the new legislation. An individual agent's utility function is given by

$$u_i(\mu_{\gamma i}, \alpha_i, \tau) = -(\mu_{\gamma i} - \alpha_i)^2 - p_\gamma(x - \alpha_i)^2 - c_{\gamma\tau}(\alpha_i)^2 + \beta W(\alpha_i) \quad (2.8)$$

where $\mu_{\gamma i}$ is the ideal policy position for the individual i and x is the policy location of the proposed legislation. Both lie anywhere on the real line. Each agent chooses an action, α_i, which again lies on the real line. The distance $|x - \alpha_i|$ is the measure of a person's lack of compliance, which has a proportional penalty attached, due to sanctioning from first-, second-, and third-party enforcement. The magnitude of the penalty is dependent upon the prevailing state of agent relations γ, i.e. the portion of the population playing update. On the other hand, compliance itself is costly since it requires adjustment away from the status quo. These costs, denoted here by the function $c_{\gamma\tau}(.)$ are dependent upon the state of agent relations γ, the length of the legislation τ, and the difference between the policy location of the original legislation, i.e the status quo that is normalized to be 0, and the chosen action α_i.

W, since realized in the second period, is discounted by the factor β, which represents the impatience of the populace. In our two-period formulation of the game, the adjustment cost is incurred by the agents in the first period only. We do not model any strategic interaction in the second period explicitly. Instead, we make the simplifying assumption that the socially optimal decision will be made in period 2 given the information revealed in period 1. By introducing a term that captures the value generated by revealed information in the form of the socially optimal decision and including it in the objective functions of the agents, we abstract away from modeling future periods repeatedly.

Rewriting the function above with $d = x - \alpha_i$, which is the distance between the new legislation and the actual action chosen by an agent, and which can be interpreted as the level of disobedience, we get

$$u_i(\mu_{\gamma i}, d_i, \tau) = -(\mu_{\gamma i} - x + d_i)^2 - p_\gamma(d_i)^2 - c_{\gamma\tau}(x - d_i) - \beta W(x - d_i) \tag{2.9}$$

Let $c_{\gamma\tau}$ be a quadratic cost function, consisting of both fixed and marginal costs of moving away from the status quo

$$c_{\gamma\tau}(\alpha_i) = a_{\gamma\tau} + b_{\gamma\tau}\alpha_i^2 = a_{\gamma\tau} + b_{\gamma\tau}(x - d_i)^2 \tag{2.10}$$

We substitute in 2.10 and get

$$-(\mu_{\gamma i} - x + d_i)^2 - p_\gamma(d_i)^2 - a_{\gamma\tau} - b_{\gamma\tau}(x - d_i)^2 - \beta W(x - d_i) \tag{2.11}$$

Maximizing gives an individual optimal level of d_i

$$d_i = \frac{x - \mu_{\gamma i}}{1 + p_\gamma + b_{\gamma\tau}} + \frac{b_{\gamma\tau}x}{1 + p_\gamma + b_{\gamma\tau}} - \frac{1}{2(1 + p_\gamma + b_{\gamma\tau})}\beta W_\alpha \tag{2.12}$$

where W_α is the partial derivative of W with respect to α.

Now, looking at the expression for optimal disobedience chosen, we can clearly see the various forces at play. First and foremost, as expected, disobedience is higher, the further away the new policy is from the agent's preferred position. But the penalty p_γ exerts a downward pressure on this response. More importantly, the second term in the expression suggests disobedience is higher the more radical the policy is, i.e. the further away it is from the status quo. But again, the effects are dampened by the penalty imposed. The marginal cost of obedience, $b_{\gamma\tau}$, has a significant influence on it as well. Particularly, as

$$\frac{\partial}{\partial b_{\gamma\tau}}\left[\frac{b_{\gamma\tau}}{1 + p_\gamma + b_{\gamma\tau}}\right] > 0 \tag{2.13}$$

disobedience is higher if the marginal cost of compliance is higher. The last term indicates that the higher the marginal value of information revealed by first period obedience, the lower will be disobedience.

The location of the state of agent relations γ affects the agent's disobedience in three ways. First, updates in intra- and interagent relations increase the amount of guilt and disapproval or other sanctioning for disobedience. Penalty p_γ then, increases as the replicator moves toward ϑ where agents are playing the profile (U, U). Second, updates in intra- and interagent relations increase the amount of pride and approval or other benefits for obedience. The cost of compliance $c_{\gamma\tau}$ decreases as the replicator moves toward ϑ. Lastly, updates shift the ideal policy position toward new legislation. That is, the distance $|x - \mu_\gamma|$ decreases as γ approaches ϑ. Otherwise, if γ is in the vicinity of κ and no updating prevails, existing levels of intra- and interagent relations remain unchanged, and p_γ, $b_{\gamma\tau}$ and $|x - \mu_\gamma|$ remain unchanged.

Integrating over the whole distribution of individual choices gives the aggregate d for any given distribution, among agents, of ideal policy positions μ. For any given distribution of μ, say $f(\mu)$, the aggregate level of noncompliance is given by

$$\bar{d} = \int d_i f(\mu)\, d\mu \qquad (2.14)$$

Note that since integration is a linear operation, the various parameters effect d the same way as discussed above for individual d_i.

2.2.3 Legislature's Optimal Timing Rule

Given the agents' anticipated aggregate disobedience level $\bar{d}$, the legislators respond by minimizing transaction costs, i.e maximizing the objective function

$$v(\tau, \bar{d}) = -\phi_\tau |x| - \delta \psi_\tau |\bar{d}| + \delta V(x - \bar{d}) \qquad (2.15)$$

The first term indicates the enactment cost of the proposed legislation which is directly proportional to the absolute distance from the status quo. The second term, discounted at rate $\delta \in (0, 1)$, is the future extension or repeal costs, which we generally refer to as legislative maintenance costs. Let ψ_τ be a quadratic cost function, consisting of both fixed and marginal costs of maintaining legislation with respect to the aggregate compliance level

$$\psi_\tau|\bar{d}| = y_\tau + q_\tau + (z_\tau - r_\tau)\bar{d}^2 \qquad (2.16)$$

The fixed portion represents transaction costs that are independent of compliance and include such costs as adhering to rules that stipulate legislative voting procedures or presentment of the legislation before the executive. These costs are constitutionally fixed and increase linearly in the number of times that the legislation is extended or repealed. Each fixed cost extension or repeal is normalized to be 1. Since permanent legislation cannot be extended, fixed extension costs $y_1 = 0$ by definition. On the other hand, temporary legislation can either expire or be extended one or more times, and $y_0 \geq 0$. Both temporary and permanent legislation may be repealed, therefore fixed repeal costs $q_\tau \leq 1$.[15] The marginal portion of ψ_τ represents those costs dependent upon the aggregate compliance level attained in period 1, where z_τ denotes extension costs and r_τ denotes repeal costs. Because permanent legislation cannot be extended, $z_1 = 0$ by definition. Lastly, the third term of equation 2.16 represents the value of revealed information in making an optimal decision in period 2. This again is a function of aggregate compliance $\bar{d}$.

We want to focus on the choice between temporary or permanent legislation for any given new policy x. The legislature chooses the optimal τ, from the two possible values 0 or 1. We denote 0 as the decision to legislate temporarily, and 1 as the decision to legislate permanently. Hence, the legislators will choose to legislate temporarily if

$$-\phi_0|x| - \delta\psi_0|\bar{d}| + \delta V(x - \bar{d}) > -\phi_1|x| - \delta\psi_1|\bar{d}| + \delta V(x - \bar{d}) \qquad (2.17)$$

Substitute in equation 2.10 and get

15 Legislation cannot be repealed twice. If the same legislation is reenacted and repealed at some point in the future it is understood as new legislation and n is reset.

$$-\phi_0|x| - \delta(y_0 + q_0 + (z_0 - r_0)\bar{d}^2) + \delta V(x - \bar{d}) >$$
$$-\phi_1|x| - \delta(y_1 + q_1 + (z_1 - r_1)\bar{d}^2) + \delta V(x - \bar{d}) \qquad (2.18)$$

2.3 COMPARING WELFARE

As mentioned above, the location of agent relations γ in Markov state space affects the penalty, the marginal cost of compliance, and the location of the ideal policy position. Each of these affect aggregate compliance. For example, when γ approaches the update profile basin ϑ, the penalty is increased, the marginal cost of compliance is decreased, and the ideal policy position moves toward the location of the new legislation. Compliance is therefore increased, and thus the overall value of information revealed regarding the optimal location of the legislation is increased. This plays a significant role in the legislature's strategic choice. The legislature induces higher levels of compliance by passing new legislation that updates agent relations, but is only able to realize that value under a temporary timing rule. At the same time, new legislation may fail to update agent relations and may require high fixed extension costs. We begin by characterizing the optimal timing rule when legislation fails to update agent relations.

Proposition 1 *If the profile $(-U,-U)$ of the agent relations game obtains in dominant strategies, social welfare is maximized with permanent timing rules when the difference in permanent and temporary enactment costs are less than any potential savings of permanent maintenance costs, i.e.* $(\phi_1 - \phi_0)|x| < \delta y_0$. *Social welfare is maximized with temporary timing rules when* $(\phi_1 - \phi_0)|x| > \delta y_0$, *and either timing rule maximizes social welfare when* $(\phi_1 - \phi_0)|x| = \delta y_0$.[16]

When $(-U,-U)$ obtains in dominant strategies, the location of agent relations γ is κ. Agent relations within the population do not undergo updating, and existing levels of guilt, pride, disapproval, approval and other costs and benefits prevail, irrespective of new legislation. Therefore, penalty p_γ and the marginal cost of

[16] All proofs are given in the appendix to this chapter.

compliance $b_{\gamma\tau}$ remain unchanged. The location of the ideal policy position μ_γ remains unchanged as well. It follows that agent utility and aggregate compliance levels remain unaffected by new legislation, and that marginal maintenance costs $(z_\tau - r_\tau)$ remain at existing levels for both temporary and permanent legislation. However, the fixed portion of maintenance costs can differ. When temporary legislation is extended at least once, $y_0 > 0$, and fixed maintenance costs for temporary timing rules are strictly greater than fixed maintenance of permanent timing rules. Legislators therefore are faced with the choice between any additional costs of enacting legislation permanently instead of temporarily, and any potential cost savings of permanent maintenance. When the difference in enactment costs is less than any fixed temporary extension costs, social welfare is maximized with a permanent timing rule.

Corollary 2 *If Γ is a coordination game with payoffs $(a > c, d > b)$ and the stationary state of agent relations γ is within the basin $[\iota, 1)$, social welfare is maximized with permanent timing rules as $\lambda \to 0$ and when $(\phi_1 - \phi_0)|x| < \delta y_0$. Social welfare is maximized with temporary timing rules as $\lambda \to 0$ and when $(\phi_1 - \phi_0)|x| > \delta y_0$, and either timing rule maximizes social welfare as $\lambda \to 0$ and $(\phi_1 - \phi_0)|x| = \delta y_0$.*

Proposition 3 *If the profile (U, U) obtains in dominant strategies, social welfare is maximized with temporary timing rules when any savings in marginal maintenance costs plus the difference in permanent and temporary enactment costs are greater than temporary fixed maintenance costs, i.e. $-\delta z_0 \bar{d}^2 + (\phi_1 - \phi_0)|x| < \delta y_0$. Social welfare is maximized with permanent timing rules when $-\delta z_0 \bar{d}^2 + (\phi_1 - \phi_0)|x| > \delta y_0$, and either timing rule maximizes social welfare when $-\delta z_0 \bar{d}^2 + (\phi_1 - \phi_0)|x| = \delta y_0$.*

When (U, U) obtains in dominant strategies, the location of agent relations γ is ϑ. Agent relations in the population undergo updating, and the existing levels of guilt, pride, disapproval, approval and other costs and benefits increase. Therefore, penalty p_γ, which exerts a downward pressure on optimal disobedience, increases; the marginal cost of compliance $b_{\gamma\tau}$, which exerts an upward pressure on optimal disobedience, decreases. The distribution of ideal policy positions μ_γ, also in response to updating, shifts toward the location of new legislation. This shift decreases the absolute distance $x - \mu_\gamma$, which dampens disobedience. It follows that agent utility and aggregate compliance levels increase, and unlike the scenario where no updating takes place, marginal maintenance costs are affected.

Now marginal maintenance costs are affected for both permanent and temporary timing rules, but permanent legislation can not be extended. This means that permanent legislation only realizes any effect from an increase in aggregate compliance for repeals, while temporary legislation realizes any effect for extensions and repeals. Particularly, an increase in compliance increases marginal repeal costs r_τ, but decreases marginal extension costs z_0. Therefore, temporary marginal maintenance costs are strictly less than permanent marginal maintenance costs when aggregate compliance $\bar{d}$ increases. However, since a temporary timing rule can require multiple extensions, fixed temporary maintenance costs are weakly greater than fixed permanent maintenance costs. As a result, social welfare is maximized with temporary timing rules when any savings in marginal maintenance costs plus any savings in temporary enactment costs are greater than any additional fixed extension costs. Otherwise, if numerous extensions are sufficiently costly, social welfare is maximized when legislators forgo the savings of that portion of extensions costs which are dependent upon $\bar{d}$ and, legislate once and for all with a permanent timing rule.

Corollary 4 *If Γ is a coordination game with payoffs $(a > c, d > b)$ and the stationary state of agent relations γ is within the basin $(\iota, 0]$, social welfare is maximized with temporary timing rules as $\lambda \rightarrow 0$ and when $-\delta z_0 \bar{d}^2 + (\phi_1 - \phi_0)|x| < \delta y_0$. Social welfare is maximized with permanent timing rules as $\lambda \rightarrow 0$ and when $-\delta z_0 \bar{d}^2 + (\phi_1 - \phi_0)|x| > \delta y_0$, and either timing rule maximizes social welfare as $\lambda \rightarrow 0$ and when $-\delta z_0 \bar{d}^2 + (\phi_1 - \phi_0)|x| = \delta y_0$.*

2.4 DISCUSSION

The preceding analysis demonstrates how agent relations influence a population's choice of compliance, and how the consequence of that choice affects the legislature's strategic decision to legislate temporarily or permanently. The analysis highlights an important dimension of the timing rule decision that has been unaddressed in the literature, namely the residual effects of a temporary policy.

Legislation can update agent relations and increase compliance levels after the law has expired.

It may be rare that temporary legislation so decisively moves a population to an update or no update equilibrium. For this reason, we show that the results still hold when the agents are in a basin of attraction near either equilibrium. Imitation moves them toward a state in which everyone plays (U) or ($-U$) as a best response amongst each other, and once they are in the vicinity of either of these equilibria, they will tend to stay there. The legislator's best response in this scenario is nearly the same as when everyone plays (U) or ($-U$) in dominant strategies.[17] There are two additional elements in her decision, however: (i) how likely is movement away from the stationary state and (ii) how long will movement take.

As a Markov process, the likelihood from moving from any given state to another is strictly positive. This is verified by noting that in any state, there is a positive probability after learning has occurred that all players are drawn to be mutants and choose the strategy that gives the new state in question. How long it takes for the population to move from one equilibrium to the other, or from any point $\gamma(0)$ to any equilibrium, depends on how quickly learning proceeds and how soon it leads to consistent behavior. This in turn depends on three aspects of the new law.

First, to what extent does the law reinforce what has governed intra- and interagent relations in the past? A large deviation from existing levels of internal cost and benefit bases for noncompliant and compliant behavior may be more difficult to learn. Similarly, it may be more difficult to adjust to a large deviation from existing levels of willingness to sanction or reward others for noncompliance and compliance. Gradual adjustments to the law, and hence to what is required of agent relations for compliance, may increase the pace of learning. Second, learning will be faster the more intelligible and simpler is the new law. When agents are vaguely aware of a substantive legal change, or cannot process it easily due to its complexity, the length of time required to update to optimal agent relations may be very long. To this end, direct and simple communication from lawmakers can eliminate the need for people to learn new sanction and reward levels from each other, which can take

17 It is precisely the same as λ goes to 0.

additional iterations of the game to process. Simpler behaviors may be learned more quickly for similar reasons. Generally, learning will proceed faster when less accumulation of experience at playing the game is required to arrive at an optimal level of agent relations. Lastly, the more important the law is to the players the more likely they will commit their decision-making resources toward socially interacting around its substance. Consideration of what level of internal costs and benefits one assigns to a behavior, or learning what level of costs and benefits other agents assign to a behavior, is more likely to occur for behaviors that the agent considers consequential.

2.5 CONCLUSION

We have considered the impact of post-expiration effects on the choice of a temporary or permanent timing rule. Although permanent statutes can be repealed and temporary statutes can be extended, each allocates legislation costs differently. This difference permits legislators to optimize on the choice of timing rule when legislation produces residual effects, which we have generally described as updates in agent relations. Updates increase compliance, which in turn, reveals more information about the optimal location of the legislation for both agents and legislators.

When agents do not undergo updating, the costs of complying with temporary and permanent legislation are the same and the optimal location of legislation remains the same. However, the fixed costs of legislating temporarily are weakly greater than the fixed costs of legislating permanently since temporary legislation may require numerous extensions. In this case, legislators weigh the difference in permanent and temporary enactment costs against fixed temporary extension costs, and maximize social welfare by choosing the timing rule that minimizes costs.

When agents undergo updating, compliance is less costly for both legislation types and the optimal location of legislation changes. Marginal maintenance costs are decreased, but only temporary timing rules can benefit from the reduction in cost. In this case, legislators maximize social welfare by weighing any savings in temporary marginal maintenance costs plus any savings in temporary enactment costs against fixed temporary extension costs.

More generally, this chapter contributes to a growing body of literature on timing rules. While previous theories have demonstrated the usage of timing rules in uncertain regulatory environments in order to minimize transactions cost, our theory demonstrates their general usage to minimize transactions cost, especially where legal impact is certain, but agent adaptation is gradual.

APPENDIX

Proof of Proposition 1

Legislators are faced with the decision

$$-\phi_0|x| - \delta(y_0 + q_0 + (z_0 - r_0)\bar{d}^2) + \delta V(x - \bar{d}) \gtreqless$$
$$-\phi_1 x - \delta(y_1 + q_1 + (z_1 - r_1)\bar{d}^2) + \delta V(x - \bar{d})$$

Recall that an agent chooses disobedience such that

$$d_i = \frac{x - \mu_{\gamma i}}{1 + p_\gamma + b_{\gamma\tau}} + \frac{b_{\gamma\tau}x}{1 + p_\gamma + b_{\gamma\tau}} - \frac{1}{2(1 + p_\gamma + b_{\gamma\tau})}\beta W_\alpha$$

and that aggregate disobedience is given by $\bar{d} = \int d_i f(\mu)\, d\mu$, for any distribution of ideal policy positions. Because the profile $(-U, -U)$ obtains in dominant strategies, the location of normative relations γ is κ and p_γ and $b_{\gamma\tau}$ remain unchanged by definition. Moreover, as agent relations are not updated, ideal position positions μ_γ remain unchanged. This implies that $(z_0 - r_0)\bar{d}^2 = (z_1 - r_0)\bar{d}^2$. Because the fixed cost of a repeal is the same for temporary and permanent legislation, $q_0 = q_1$, and because permanent legislation cannot be extended, $y_1 = 0$.

Legislators are therefore faced with

$$-\phi_0|x| - \delta(y_0) \gtreqless -\phi_1|x|$$

and maximize social welfare by setting $\tau = 1$ when $(-\phi_1 + \phi_0)|x| < -\delta y_0$, $\tau = 0$ when $(-\phi_1 + \phi_0)|x| > -\delta y_0$, and $\tau = 1$ or 0 when $(-\phi_1 + \phi_0)|x| = -\delta y_0$. □

Proof of Proposition 3

Because the profile (U, U) obtains in dominant strategies, the location of agent relations γ is ϑ. Therefore, the penalty p_γ increases and the marginal cost of compliance $b_{\gamma\tau}$ decreases by assumption. Recall that an agent chooses disobedience such that

$$d_i = \frac{x - \mu_{\gamma i}}{1 + p_\gamma + b_{\gamma\tau}} + \frac{b_{\gamma\tau}x}{1 + p_\gamma + b_{\gamma\tau}} - \frac{1}{2(1 + p_\gamma + b_{\gamma\tau})}\beta W_\alpha$$

Clearly, an increase in p_γ decreases disobedience. And since

$$\frac{\partial}{\partial b_{\gamma\tau}}\left[\frac{b_{\gamma\tau}}{1 + p_\gamma + b_{\gamma\tau}}\right] > 0$$

a decrease in $b_{\gamma\tau}$ also decreases disobedience. By assumption, the location of γ at ϑ shifts the ideal policy $\mu_{\gamma i}$ towards the new legislation x. This means that the distance $|x - \mu_{\gamma i}|$ decreases and as a result, disobedience d_i decreases. It follows that aggregate disobedience, given by $\bar{d} = \int d_i f(\mu)\, d\mu$, decreases for profile $\{U, U\}$.

Legislators are faced with the decision

$$-\phi_0|x| - \delta(y_0 + q_0 + (z_0 - r_0)\bar{d}^2) + \delta V(x - \bar{d}) \gtreqless$$

$$-\phi_1|x| - \delta(y_1 + q_1 + (z_1 - r_1)\bar{d}^2) + \delta V(x - \bar{d})$$

Aggregate disobedience $\bar{d}$ effects both $(z_0 - r_0)$ and $(z_1 - r_1)$, but recall that $z_1 = 0$ because permanent legislation is not extended by definition. In contrast, $z_0 \geq 0$.

Now decreasing $\bar{d}$ increases the absolute value of both marginal repeal costs r_0 and r_1. Therefore, $-\delta(z_0 - r_0) \leq -\delta(z_1 - r_1)$.

Because the fixed cost of a repeal is the same for temporary and permanent legislation, $q_0 = q_1$, and because permanent legislation cannot be extended, $y_1 = 0$.

Legislators are therefore faced with

$$-\phi_0\, x - \delta y_0 - \delta z_0\bar{d}^2 \gtreqless -\phi_1\, x$$

and maximize social welfare by setting $\tau = 0$ when $-\delta z_0\bar{d}^2 + (\phi_1 - \phi_0)|x| < \delta y_0$, $\tau = 1$ when $-\delta z_0\bar{d}^2 + (\phi_1 - \phi_0)|x| > \delta y_0$, $\tau = 0$ or 1 when $-\delta z_0\bar{d}^2 + (\phi_1 - \phi_0)|x| = \delta y_0$. □

3. Long-term residual effects

> Legislators, therefore, ought not to trust the future government of a state entirely to chance, but ought to provide a system of laws to regulate the administration of public affairs to the latest posterity. Effects will always correspond to causes; and wise regulations, in any commonwealth, are the most valuable legacy that can be left to future ages.
>
> David Hume ([1740] 1882: 19)

3.1 INTRODUCTION

In the previous chapter legislators choose to legislate permanently or temporarily based upon transaction cost minimization for short- to medium-term compliance benefits. However, in addition to short- to medium-term compliance benefits, legislators can benefit from long-term compliance that results from the creation of social norms. The present chapter considers the choice between temporary and permanent legislation when this additional benefit is specified in the objective function of legislators. That legislators can create social norms differs from the current law and economics norms research which emphasizes the legislator's passive role in norm creation. In that literature, legislators create laws for compliance benefits which, in turn, create (or focalize) social norms (Cooter 1998, 2000, McAdams 2000b,a, McAdams and Rasmusen 2005, Feldman 2009). Emphasis is placed upon the law's role in norm creation. In some cases however, legislators are directly legislating social norms.[1] This is especially visible when legislators nearing retirement could legislate temporarily and save transactions cost, but instead choose to legislate permanently in an attempt to extend normative influence beyond their lawmaking careers.[2]

[1] Thus the process is referred to as "expressive law" or the "expressive function of law," and legislators are separated from a norm entrepreneurial role, though Carbonara et al. (2008) is an exception.

[2] In some cases interest groups might make immediate material

Under plausible conditions, permanent legislation is more costly than temporary legislation. When there is no probability of extension and no probability of repeal, permanent legislation provides an infinite stream of benefits, while temporary legislation provides only a discrete stream of benefits. Holding the substance of the legislation and other factors constant, the value of permanent legislation is strictly greater than that of temporary legislation, where the difference is reflected in the length of the temporary period and the demand-side discount factor. If legislators are paying for a policy in benefits, permanent legislation is more costly than temporary legislation (Gersen 2007).

In this setting, benefits vary only with respect to the number of years that the policy is in effect. Because temporary legislation lasts for less time and produces fewer benefits, it is likely to be less costly than permanent legislation. With a succession of extensions, however, temporary and permanent legislation benefit levels can equate. Moreover, as shown in proposition 3, extension costs can decrease in response to increased first- and second-party enforcement when legislation is expressive. If permanent legislation is more costly because it provides a lengthier stream of compliance benefits, and temporary legislation can more efficiently pay for those benefits because, for example, the extension costs of expressive legislation are decreasing, then legislators may choose a permanent timing rule for expressive legislation in exchange for benefits beyond short- to medium-term compliance. As mentioned above, the decision to legislate permanently is especially striking when the benefits that flow from legislation extend beyond the careers of legislators.

In order to explain the choice of permanent legislation when temporary legislation appears more efficient in a short- to medium-term transactions cost framework, we account for a longer-term compliance benefit. Permanent legislation can produce a marginally stronger expressive effect which, in turn, leads to a higher level of long-term norm creation. Legislators are willing to pay higher costs for a permanent timing rule since the benefit of norm creation may

---

transfers to those legislators in exchange for permanent legislation, but in others, legislators may receive a nonmaterial benefit that takes the form of the knowledge of leaving a normative legacy. This chapter focuses on the latter. Chapter 7 elaborates further on the role of interest group transfers.

be increased, or more expected, in relation to what would otherwise occur with a series of temporary enactments. All of this depends on the legislator's ability to create social norms through lawmaking. The following section provides a short background on social norms scholarship, and describes the dominant law and economics paradigm, i.e. the norm market. The norm market is then expanded in section 3.3 to demonstrate how voluntary decision-based compliance can develop into involuntary nondecision-based compliance. The model explains several types of compliance that vary with respect to the volition of the agents, and each is related to the degree of normative legacy available to the legislator that can be effected through legislative enactment.

3.2 SOCIAL NORMS

Background

Compliance as a managerial concept emerged when legal theorists began to question the role of law in the modern administrative state. They observed that increases in specialization and competition led to increases in inequality, which if remaining unchecked, were thought to eventually give way to disorder. Legislative lawmaking, and its ability to demarcate compliant and noncompliant behavior with formalized rules, came to be seen as set in place for correcting market failures and redistributing benefits to preserve the market institution and uphold order. This view supported the expansion of legally regulated activities on the basis of accommodating conflict, normalizing division, and depoliticizing instability and unrest.[3]

While many agreed that achieving these goals was normatively desirable from the standpoint of public interest, public choice

---

[3] Michel Foucault elaborates on how the function of coercion that characterized early legal systems has largely been displaced with the function of normalizing behavior that characterizes modern legal systems in his *History of Sexuality*: "I do not mean to say that the law fades into the background or that the institutions of justice tend to disappear, but rather that the law operates more and more as a norm, and that the judicial institution is increasingly incorporated into a continuum of apparatuses (medical, administrative, and so on) whose functions are for the most part regulatory" (Foucault 1990: 144).

scholars interpreted the pretext of conserving order or stability as a concealment of rational choice motivations. Legislators and regulators, in their efforts to defuse public conflicts arising from competition, were at once resolving their own competitive conflicts and advancing their own private interests.[4] Public choice scholarship found private interest motives entangled with public interest legislation, and demonstrated that entanglement throughout history.

The evolution of royal law institutions in medieval England, for example, could be seen as driven by the king's concern for law and order on the one hand, but also by the king's concern for raising revenues through expanding his jurisdiction.[5] The expansion of the number of felonious offenses in which property escheated to the king, the demise of the lex mercatoria which led to increased fees for common law judges, and even the adoption of the Magna Carta which reestablished the barons' feudal right to confiscate felons' land, could all be seen from a dual perspective. Each could be treated as motivated by public interest, but also as motivated by the private interests of its proponents. From the same perspective, one can interpret Foucault's observation – that the coercive function of law as a tool of sovereignty has been displaced with the new function of normalizing behavior and stabilizing society through regulation – as simply motivated by rational choice considerations of the beneficiaries of societal normalization and stability.

Yet whether the function of regulatory law is to normalize and stabilize societal unrest, or to maximize private interests of lawmakers, the deterrence model no longer conveyed the most credible explanation for obedience to the law. In the modern context, both sides saw that increases in the law's informalness could lead to increases in the law's effectiveness, and found that compliance theories placed an exaggerated importance on severity of punishment and probability of detection. Theorists began to recognize that proclamation of prescriptive rules, without threat of punishment, was enough to modify behavior, especially when those rules embodied prevailing societal norms. Even within law and economics, whose price-theoretic tradi-

---

4 James Buchanan explains that while modern economics tasked itself with analyzing and proscribing for market failures, the public choice project did the same for political failures (Buchanan 1975: 172).

5 See Lyon (1980: 52–63), and generally, Benson (1990) at chapter 3.

tion naturally embraces expected punishment explanations of compliance, a large project developed to explain the interaction between social norms and the law.

Many law and economics scholars were interested in this question because they felt that understanding the interaction between social norms and the law could reduce the size of the regulatory state. Perhaps the most well known study is Ellickson (1991), which describes several groups which settle disputes without relying on the formalities of law. Instead, they rely on approval and disapproval logics rooted in social custom. Cooter (2000) went a step further by articulating a theory without relying on external social relations like those in Ellickson. Citing Kohlberg, Piaget, and other psychologists, he stressed that individuals who have internalized the norm of obedience to law will internalize the specific behavioral obligations embodied in a law, since guilt costs are reflected in their preference for obedience.

Most scholarship now reflects that law operates in modalities beyond the Austinian model of commands and coercion. It contends that there is an expressive effect of law which motivates human behavior separate from, or in addition to, a severity-detection calculus. Scholars who have noted the effect acknowledge that rules are integral parts of social processes that prompt self-regulation on the part of the regulated group, either through stabilizing existing patterns of normative behavior, or through transforming widespread ideas of what is the appropriate mode of interaction.[6]

Following these advances, state of the art compliance theories now account for both tangible and intangible motivations that influence behavior.[7] In addition to the material costs and benefits associated with behavior, these theories stress that moral obligation and social influence are fundamental determinants of regulatory outcomes, which can exist independently of a strictly materialist causality. Today, compliance is understood as a result of some mix between regulatory deterrence on the one hand, and relational obligation, socialization, reputation, legitimacy, and other phenomena stemming from social interaction on the other hand.

In the previous chapter, internalized social norms are understood to impose a cost on or confer a benefit to individuals. The costs

---

6 See above 2.2.1, which models this transformation.

7 See for example Sutinen and Kuperan (1999).

and benefits impact their decision to comply with a norm, which is reflected in the level of compliance (with the law) observed by legislators. Toward identifying a potential long-term benefit of permanent legislation, we now consider a further class of internalized norms, where an individual's cost–benefit calculus is not consciously performed. Much of internal compliance often appears contrary to an individual's interests, and theories that rely on a static form of utility maximization continue to be plagued by nonconsequentialist objections as the norms and law research project progresses.[8] By adopting a dynamic and graduated view of norm development, we are able to construct a rational-choice model for all normative compliance, even for that compliance which appears to be outside of an individual's utility calculus.[9]

As in chapter 2, the following sections assume that legislation effects normative behavior. Several empirical studies support this claim. Messell (1968) describes how the Soviet leadership used the law to engineer revolution in Central Asia without relying on formal enforcement, Funk (2007) found that abolition of a symbolic fine for not voting reduced voter turnout, and Feldman (2009) demonstrated in an experiment that persons who are primed with legal expression comply with trade secret laws.[10] Each provides evidence that supports the claim that the law affects that behavior which is mediated by social norms. In addition to assuming an expressive effect of law, the following section defines legislators or interest groups who demand

---

[8] For example, Kofford and Miller (2007: 21) state that "Sociologists and organization theorists have studied how habit, custom, and norms determine social outcomes. Although economic systems are really just a type of social organization, economists have neglected these factors. There is a good reason why: they generally lie outside the realm of the rational maximization model that economists use." Eric Posner (2007: x) concedes that "economists had had a great deal of trouble understanding why people would comply with social norms when it was not in their self-interest to do so."

[9] The types of norms discussed are not conventions as in Lewis (1969), such as driving on the right-hand side of the road. Conventions in this sense imply the cognitive use of higher-order expectations, i.e. I expect that you expect that I expect, etc. However, it is obvious that driving on the other side incurs an expected cost. Thus convention norms enter into a utility calculus.

[10] Feldman's study is of special note as he primes the subjects with three types of legal expression: price-related, consensus-related, and morality-related. He finds that morality-related expression has the largest impact on compliance.

legislation which has an expressive effect as norm entrepreneurs. Most law and economics scholarship takes legal expression literally; it is the law or the state that expresses normative judgment. Here, the human agency of legal expression is emphasized. Legislators or the groups that they represent are understood to reflect their subjective normative opinions and function as norm entrepreneurs.

Section 3.3 shows that norms initially supported by legislators can exist independently of first- and second-party enforcement after a sufficient number of periods. This is accomplished by supposing that increases in time lead to decreases in guilt, pride, disapproval, and approval due to forgetfulness. Existing levels of normative compliance are maintained, or even increased, however, because habit serves as an additional source of compliance. The intuition behind this claim is predicated upon the concept of tradition, where older traditions are often more intensely observed. Similarly, older norms have greater ability to actuate habitual observance. Thus there is a possibility that over time, second-party and first-party enforcement peter out without an attendant disappearance of the norm. Compliance that occurs during this time period is what we refer to as the long-term normative effect of expressive legislation.

3.2.1 The Norm Consumer

The basic theory of economic behavior states that

$$U_i = U_i(A_1, \ldots, A_m)$$

is the utility function of the *i*th individual, and that $A_1, \ldots, A_m$ are her basic commodities or wants. These can be objectified as a few basic wants like food, clothing and shelter. Marshall mentions a few non-basic wants like variety and distinction, which can also be suggested by A.[11]

Each individual employs a set of production functions that determine how much each of the commodities can be produced with her available resources:

$$A_j = f_j^i(x_j, t_j, F^i, S_j^1, \ldots, S_j^r)$$

---

[11] Marshall (1961) Book 3, chapter 2.

where x_j are quantities of various market goods and services; t_j are quantities of time; F^i are environmental variables like i's experience and education which govern her first-party enforcement through guilt and pride; and $S_j^1, \ldots, S_j^r$ are prevailing levels of second-party enforcement through disapproval or approval of other individuals that affect her own output of the commodities that drive her utility. For example, if A_1 describes i's standing amongst her students, $S_j^1, \ldots, S_j^r$ are the opinions of her held by each r student.

These are usually taken as outside of i's control and consequently taken as given. Following Becker (1996a), we assume the contrary, that is, that i can change S_j with her own effort. For example, she can take her students out for a drink or grade their papers generously. Or if i were interested in distinction or approval within her community, she might donate to charity, or refrain from displaying bad behavior in public. This behavior can be formulated in the production function for the $(S_j^1, \ldots, S_j^r)$ that depends partially on her efforts and partially on other variables.

Following Becker, we simplify by assuming a single commodity that is produced with a single good and a single characteristic of other individuals, ignoring i's time input and the environmental or historical factors that govern her first-party enforcement. Maximizing utility, therefore, is the same as maximizing the output of this commodity representing her interpersonal relations:[12]

$$U_i = A(x, S)$$

It is further assumed that the effect of other variables on this commodity is independent of i's own efforts. Thus, S is represented by an additive function:

$$S = D_i + e \qquad (3.1)$$

where e gives the effect of i's effort, and D_i gives the level of S when i makes no effort. As such, D_i measures i's endowed normative environment.

Her budget constraint for money income can be given by:

---

[12] If we instead ignore interpersonal relations, the commodity in question could be her intrapersonal relations as well.

$$p_x x + p_S e = M_i$$

where M_i represents her money income, where $p_s e$ is the amount she spends on S, and ps is the price she pays for one unit of S. Substitute $S - D_i$ for e in the equation above, and get:

$$p_x x + p_S S = M_i + p_S D_i = N_i$$

The right-hand side gives the sum of i's money income (M_i) and the value she assigns to her normative environment ($p_S D_i$). This will be called her norm income.[13] The left-hand side shows how her norm income is spent, partially on her own goods (x) and partially on the characteristics of others that drive their approval or disapproval of her (S).

Maximizing the utility given by $U_i = A\ (x, S)$ while subject to constraint on norm income given by the equation above, the equilibrium condition is:

$$\left(\frac{\delta U_i}{\delta_x}\right) / \left(\frac{\delta U_i}{\delta S}\right) = \frac{p_x}{p_S} \tag{3.2}$$

p_s is the monetary equivalent of the marginal utility of S when $S = D_i$ (or when $e = 0$).

Her equilibrium position is displayed in Figure 3.1, which depicts S with a positive marginal utility in the production of A. For example, S can represent the good opinions of i's neighbors. The quantity $0D$ of S measures her interpersonal normative environment, and $0x_0$ her income measured in terms of x, so that F_0 gives her utility when she spends nothing on S. This is her endowed interpersonal normative environment.

F_0N_0 measures the opportunities for purchasing additional S, and i maximizes her utility by moving along F_0N_0 to point f_0, where the slopes of the opportunity curve and her indifference curve meet. Her equilibrium purchase of interpersonal relations S is given by the line

[13] Recall that the single commodity S, the opinions of i that others hold which determine second-party enforcement, could be substituted for the commodity F, the opinion that i holds of herself which determines first-party enforcement. Thus the norm income could also be maximized to increase the output of F given that $U_i = A(x, F)$.

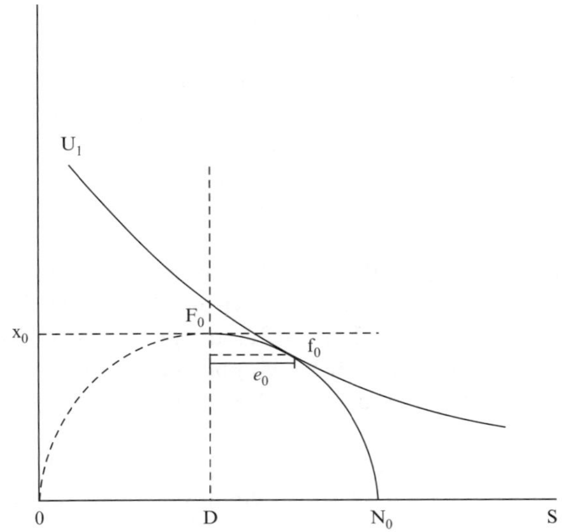

Figure 3.1 *Equilibrium purchases of interpersonal relations S, with money income x*

segment e_0, which clearly depicts a reduction in x, her money income. The following section examines the production of S in detail.

3.2.2 The Norm Producer

The process of social norm creation begins when norm entrepreneurs make their first normative statement. By normative statement, Habermas' general notion of a validity claim is useful for explication. Validity claims are claims that enter public discourse, and are debated in public life. Successful claims, that is, those claims that become valid after debate in the public sphere, are those that survive objections and become rationalized (Habermas 1984: 10–15). For instance, a norm entrepreneur may make one or more validity claims asserting that *i* ought not to practice abortion. He may claim that abortion is unnatural, and morally wrong, or that it is medically unsound in less-developed countries. There is a public debate on these claims, perhaps ongoing, where the norm entrepreneur makes his claims. A successful claim for *i* is defined as a claim that *i* validates, and rationalizes after debating it. Once rationalized, the claim affects *i*'s intrapersonal utility, which in turn can induce compliance.[14] Norm entrepreneurs make claims in order to influence and persuade persons to validate and rationalize a normative statement. When a person rationalizes a normative claim, their utility from compliance with that claim increases, and their utility from non-compliance decreases.

Entrepreneurs establish norms by expressing a claim more often, or by intensifying it. For example, if the norm producer wants to establish a new security norm, he may more frequently claim that there is a terrorist threat, or intensify that claim, say, by asserting that terrorists have new and more dangerous capabilities. The expressive function of law also functions as a validity claim. Thus the passage of new security measures, such as those found in the USA PATRIOT Act, may function as a claim to the existence or seriousness of a terrorist threat. Norm entrepreneurs, who build income sources by compelling *i* to spend her income on compliance, invest in increasing the level of their claims. At a particular threshold we can imagine that a validity claim, backed by a sufficient level of investment, becomes a norm.

The equilibrium price of complying with a norm changes when the level of investment made by a norm entrepreneur changes. A simple norm market can be represented by

$$Q_d = D(P)\,(dD/dP < 0)$$

$$Q_s = S(P, A_0)\,(\delta S/\delta P > 0;\, \delta S/\delta A_0 < 0)$$

where the price of adhering to a norm P, is a function of both quantity demanded and supplied, and A_0 represents the exogenously determined level of investment in claims. The partial derivative $\delta S/\delta A_0$ is negative because an increase in the level of investment A_0 increases the cost of producing a norm and lowers supply. Assuming that the equilibrium position of this market is defined by the equilibrium condition $Q_d = Q_s$, we are able to write

14 Thus the validity claim impacts her experience and education, which in turn impacts her maximization calculus with respect to first-party enforcement. Likewise, if she interacts with another person relative to the entrepreneurial claim, her social relations are impacted which in turn effects her maximization of second-party enforcement.

$$D(P) - S(P, A_0) = 0$$

By the implicit-function theorem the equilibrium condition can be taken to be an identity in some neighborhood of the equilibrium solution[15]

$$D(\overline{P}) - S(\overline{P}, A_0) \equiv 0$$

where $\overline{P} = \overline{P}(A_0)$. Taking the total derivative of this identity with respect to A_0 gives

$$\frac{dD}{d\overline{P}}\frac{\delta\overline{P}}{\delta A_0} - \frac{\delta S}{\delta\overline{P}}\frac{\delta\overline{P}}{\delta A_0} + \frac{\delta S}{\delta A_0} = 0$$

Solving for $(\delta\overline{P}/\delta A_0)$, we get

$$\frac{\delta\overline{P}}{\delta A_0} = -\frac{\delta S/\delta A_0}{dD/d\overline{P} - \delta S/\delta\overline{P}} < 0 \qquad (3.3)$$

The above solution shows that an increase (decrease) in the level of normative investment will lead to a decrease (increase) in the equilibrium price of adhering to a norm. The intuition behind the solution is that additional investment in claims made by the norm entrepreneur renders the normative behavior more validated and rationalized within *i*'s endowed normative environment, and hence less costly for *i* to follow.

Since in the equilibrium state we have $\overline{Q} = D(P)$, and since $\overline{P} = \overline{P}(A_0)$ we get

$$\frac{\delta\overline{Q}}{\delta A_0} = \frac{dD}{d\overline{P}}\frac{\delta\overline{P}}{\delta A_0} > 0 \qquad (3.4)$$

which conveys that an increase (decrease) in claims investment will lead to an increase (decrease) in the equilibrium quantity demanded. Quantity demanded increases because an increase in claims investment causes the equilibrium price to fall, which increases demand.

15 Since the derivatives of $D(P)$ and $S(P, A_0)$ are continuous, the derivatives of $F(P, A_0)$ are also continuous. Thus $F_P = dD/dP - \delta S/\delta P$ is always positive, and the implicit-function theorem applies.

Thus entrepreneurial investment in a norm raises the level of normative compliance.

3.3 FROM VOLUNTARY TO INVOLUNTARY COMPLIANCE

As mentioned above, one of the aims of this chapter is to establish a non-normative theory of norms, entirely behavioral and positivistic, that coherently demonstrates normative compliance as motivated by self-interest even when such compliance does not offer guilt and disapproval costs, or pride and approval benefits. This type of compliance is distinguished from compliance with convention since conventional behavior is still able to generate costs and benefits. The norms we have in mind are those norms which are normatively preferred, even though compliance is not the outcome of first- or second-party enforcement.

If compliance does not rely on first- or second-party enforcement due to a recent normative investment, it can rely on habitual behavior due to past normative investment made by a behaviorally motivated norm entrepreneur. Becker (1996b) defines habit as a positive relation between an individual's past compliance and present compliance. For example, smoking for the past twenty years can increase the marginal utility of smoking today.[16] Elsewhere, Becker has extended that definition to include a positive relationship between other individuals' past compliance and an individual's present compliance (Becker 1996a). In that context, he quotes Mill (1872: 484) regarding the behavior of leaders:

> It is not true that the actions even of average rulers are wholly, or anything approaching to wholly, determined by their personal interest, or even by their own opinion of their personal interest . . . I insist only on what is true of all rulers, viz., that the character and course of their actions is largely influenced (independently of personal calculations) by the habitual sentiments and feelings, the general modes of thinking

---

[16] Becker is careful to acknowledge that the time intervals between consumption periods must be sufficiently large. If a person had recently smoked a cigarette, they may not want to smoke in the immediate future. See Becker 1996b: 119.

> and acting, which prevail throughout the community of which they are members; as well as by the feelings, habits, and modes of thought which characterize the particular class in that community to which they themselves belong . . .They are also much influenced by the maxims and traditions which have descended to them from other rulers, their predecessors; which maxims and traditions have been known to retain an ascendancy during long periods, even in opposition to the private interests of the rulers for the time being.

Mill recognizes a positive relationship between the past compliance with a norm by a society or group, and the present compliance with that same norm by an individual. Even when compliance appears to be in opposition to individual material interests or the social relations that govern the present, people still can receive a net benefit from compliance. This benefit is derived from complying with the norms of past generations. Tradition norms serve as good examples. For instance, several generations of American men routinely stood and removed their hats during the performance of the national anthem at a sporting event. A person today may remove their hat because they may expect disapproval from their neighbor, but that person may also think, "my father removed his hat, my grandfather removed his hat," and so receive a benefit from complying with the social relations of their absent family.

Although compliance with tradition might occur independently of actual approval or disapproval, it can be thought of as an internal outcome governed by pride or guilt. Compliance with tradition may generate a pride benefit, or noncompliance may generate a guilt cost. But when compliance or noncompliance is unconsciously habitual, to speak of pride and guilt makes less sense.

Knowledge of alternatives

Pride and guilt for a chosen behavior are felt in relation to a behavioral alternative. One feels pride for compliance when noncompliance is an option, and feels guilt for noncompliance when compliance is an option. Instead, when behavior is unconscious, or when an alternative behavior is unimagined, such a comparison is not logically permitted. Guilt functions the same way. It is felt in relation to conscious possibility.[17]

---

[17] Anderson (2008) distinguishes between practical and nonpractical guilt. Practical guilt is felt from an action that a person could avoid, and

First- and second-party enforcement exist for the opposite reason: they place behavioral possibilities in the cognitive foreground. Thus when a person is reminded that not aborting a pregnancy is an option for example, she may feel guilt and pride when weighing the possibilities. Likewise, a reminder to recycle presents an alternative. Without knowledge of the possible recycle alternative, one could not experience a pride benefit for depositing a bottle in the recycle bin, nor incur a guilt cost for depositing a bottle in the trash. Without conscious behavioral options, pride and guilt lose their meaning, and normative behavior can appear without aim.

It is this visibly aimless compliance that rational-choice critics point to when criticizing law and economics' purely volitional approach to norms. Those critics emphasize that understanding apparently involuntary compliance as voluntary, whether it is compliance with the will of the community as is the case with norms, or with the will of the sovereign as is the case for law, "winds up doing nothing so much as reinventing the discredited jurisprudence of John Austin – along with the additional flaw that it excises the sovereign without whom even Austin's flawed theory is incoherent" (Mitchell 2007: 229). But other approaches, as with Mitchell's, jettison a potentially useful account of involuntary compliance by explaining it as, in Mitchell's words, "self-justifying," or in Elster's, "irreducible to rationality or indeed any form of optimizing mechanism" (Elster 1991: 15). Instead, our positive account of involuntary compliance avoids positing purposeful action for some class of behavior by treating its underlying preference as passively inherited. Most of the scholarship related to passive inheritance stems from sociology, particularly Durkheim, who demonstrates that "social structures," e.g. passively inherited norms, can shape the volition of an individual (Durkheim 1965).[18]

A nonrational approach to norms too quickly dismisses passive

nonpractical guilt is felt from an action that a person could not avoid, such as guilt for an ancestor's crimes. Note that both practical and nonpractical guilt require the existence of possible alternatives in the person's cognitive foreground. Even though nonpractical guilt is felt for an impossible behavioral alternative, that alternative is imagined nonetheless.

[18] This idea is further developed in Mark Granovetter's work on sociological embeddedness (Granovetter 1985). See generally, Hass (2007) at chapter 1.

inheritance, and overlooks a positive link between rational action and nonvolitional normative compliance; passively inherited norms were once actively created by the norm entrepreneur's rational motivations. Thus a dynamic account of norm development is able to demonstrate that after a sufficient amount of time normative compliance can occur, absent first- and second-party sanctioning, but not because of internalization of some unexplained endowment of metarules. Endowed metarules can be explained as the outcome of earlier normative investments. In an evolutionary account of norms that acknowledges nonvolitional compliance, the role of the norm entrepreneur is thus enhanced.

Section 3.2.1 illustrated that normative compliance can increase a person's utility. In Figure 3.1, people use their money income to purchase normative compliance when its marginal utility still exceeds that of other goods. This insight permits the elaboration of the market in section 3.2.2, in which the norm entrepreneur attempts to create norms that divert a person's money income in exchange for compliance. Equation 3.4 demonstrates that norm producers increase the demand for their norms by increasing investment in normative claims, much in the same way that other producers increase the demand for their goods through marketing campaigns and advertising. In static equilibrium, investments in normative claims lower the price of normative compliance. This in turn increases the quantity demanded of the norm, which increases the level of normative compliance. Because norm consumers are making compliance decisions based upon price, their decisionmaking is understood as purely voluntary. This static setting provides our foundation for a dynamic and positive account of involuntary compliance.

3.3.1 The Introduction of a Norm

Suppose that a person has no knowledge of an alternative behavioral possibility. That person experiences no utility from complying with normative behavior because at the moment, that normative behavior does not exist. At time $t = 0$, the norm entrepreneur invests in a new compliance good. He invests in that claim up to the point where he experiences no further return on his investment.

A higher level of investment increases the possibility that the person will rationalize a validity claim. Norm entrepreneurs give reasons as to why their claim should be supported; more strongly reasoned claims persuade a person to rationalize that claim more so than less strongly reasoned claims. Because persons value agreeable relations with themselves, they receive utility from compliance with rationalized claims. They reward themselves with pride for compliance and punish themselves with guilt for noncompliance.

Persons also value their relation with the norm entrepreneur if they personally know him. Even if they do not rationalize his claim, they may comply because they receive utility from an agreeable relationship with him. The norm entrepreneur rewards them with approval for their compliance, and punishes them with disapproval for their noncompliance. By equation 3.4, higher levels of claims investment lead to higher levels of compliance. Finally, persons value their relation with individuals other than the norm entrepreneur. When they know that a validity claim has been rationalized by another person, they receive utility from compliance with that claim if they value agreeable relations with that other person.

When a norm is introduced by a norm entrepreneur, it yields an amount of compliance throughout the community dependent upon the price of compliance, where the price is dependent upon the level of claims investment. The quantity demanded at time $t = 0$ reflects the static setting contained in sections 3.2.1 and 3.2.2, i.e. $\overline{Q} = D(P)$, where $\overline{P} = \overline{P}(A_0)$.

3.3.2 The Disappearance of Second-party Enforcement

Suppose now that the quantity demanded of the norm increases, independent of normative claims, by increases in time. At $t = 1$, the moment that equilibrium quantity demanded begins to depend upon time, norm entrepreneurs can reduce their level of claims investment and still establish the same demand level. Eventually, at time $t = 2$, norm entrepreneurs stop investing in normative claims altogether.

When a person interacts with a norm entrepreneur for the payoffs in Figure 3.2, *comply* is her dominant strategy because she receives utility from intra- or interpersonal relations or both. When she has intrapersonally validated the norm entrepreneur's claim, she receives utility from intrapersonal relations. She feels guilty for not complying with a norm that she now believes to be normatively valid. Or irrespective of what she thinks of the norm's validity, she may feel pride from complying with a traditional norm, or a norm expressed

	Comply	*Not comply*
Express	1,2	−1,−2
Not express	(2,1)	0,−1

Figure 3.2 Compliance equilibrium in the shadow of normative investment

by law. Social relations can enter her payoff function as well if she values her standing with the norm entrepreneur.[19] In short, her dominant strategy is *comply*.

However, the norm entrepreneur can observe compliance without making additional investments in normative claims. When he chooses *not express* at time $t = 2$, he expends fewer resources and thus experiences a greater net payoff. In the profile (*not express*, *comply*) there is compliance, but there is no normative investment. Even though this compliance equilibrium lacks normative investment, compliance is only possible because of the initial normative investment made in an earlier period. In Figure 3.3, first- and second-party enforcement have been put into motion, not nonvolitionally, but by the rational consideration of a norm entrepreneur attempting to divert a person's income at a previous point in time.

Now if we suppose that social relations affect a person's utility in the same way as the norm entrepreneur's validity claim, compliance can be further reduced to first-party enforcement in Nash equilibrium: see Figure 3.3.[20]

---

[19] In Figure 3.2, we make the simplifying assumption that the person ranks her preferences in accordance with the number of utility sources: π_i (*express, comply*) = intrapersonal and social reward > π_i (*not express, comply*) = intrapersonal reward only > π_i (*not express, not comply*) = intrapersonal punishment only > π_i (*express, not comply*) = intrapersonal and social punishment. Of course if the measurement of a utility source is continuous, other rankings can occur. The point is that under a reasonable set of assumptions, compliance can rationally occur independently of entrepreneurial investment in social norms.

[20] Again, the person ranks her preferences in the accordance with the number of utility sources: π_i (*second-party enforcement, comply*) = interpersonal reward > π_i (*no second-party enforcement, comply*) = no reward = π_i (*no second-party enforcement, not comply*) = no punishment > π_i (*second-party enforcement, not comply*) = interpersonal punishment. The enforcer

	Comply	*Not comply*
Second-party enforcement	1,1	−1,−1
No second-party enforcement	(2,0)	0,0

Figure 3.3 Social relations in the shadow of normative investment

After having accepted the conductorship of the New York Philharmonic, Gustav Mahler would occasionally take his entire orchestra to dinner. His consumption of those dinners is not understood without considering his consumption of social relations. Mahler maximizes utility by spending money income not on a value-neutral good like dinner, but on a good that provides utility with respect to its normative status. Members of a society which have internalized a norm to esteem generosity provide an esteem reward to Mahler's generosity if he has updated his interpersonal relations, i.e. he allows himself to experience their approval.

Suppose his first-chair violinist expends resources to make Mahler feel guilty in exchange for a dinner. The violinist ranks preferences as π (*not making Mahler guilty, dinner*) $= 2 > \pi$ (*making Mahler guilty, dinner*) $= 1 > \pi$ (*not making Mahler guilty, no dinner*) $= 0 > \pi$ (*making Mahler guilty, no dinner*) $= -1$, where the generosity norm and its ability to generate guilt was introduced at time $t = 0$ by a norm entrepreneur. Without this earlier normative investment in the creation of guilt for lack of generosity, the relation between Mahler and his violinist would not permit approval rewards and disapproval punishments to affect their utilities and the exchange must take place under different circumstances.

Thus a normative claim offers two behavioral possibilities: to comply or to not comply. Those behavioral possibilities are not endowed, but introduced earlier in time by norm entrepreneurs, and later reinforced by intrapersonal and interpersonal relations. In Nash equilibrium, costly reinforcement of claims from norm entrepreneurs and other social relations decrease as other sources of intrapersonal enforcement such as tradition increase over time.

ranks his preferences in accordance with compliance and the cost of sending a social sanction, where *no second-party enforcement*, which entails no sanctioning cost, is preferable to *enforcement*.

This implies that at the margin, the salience of noncompliant behavior begins to decrease because second parties avoid making costly normative claims less and less to economize. At $t = 2$, intrapersonal relations are sufficient for a compliance equilibrium. To not comply is not an option, even in the absence of approval or disapproval effects on utility.

3.3.3 The Disappearance of First-party Enforcement

When the final period $t = 3$ is reached, only first-party enforcement remains to be removed. Two possibilities can be considered. First, like Becker, it could be considered that a stronger habit yields a higher payoff. An individual might not be subject to second-party enforcement, but might continue to comply because of her knowledge of a social habit. Because she believes that others could socially sanction her on the basis of a norm, she continues to comply and experience higher expected utility. Instead, if she had no knowledge of the norm and her utility were derived solely from personal habit, she would simply comply, irrespective of her expectations regarding interaction with others. Compliance and noncompliance with personal habit might be modeled as a first-party reward and punishment, but the difference is that guilt and pride are missing because the norm is missing from the individual's cognitive foreground.

Equally plausible is that persons consciously eliminate first-party enforcement as maximizing behavior. Since compliance is established at $t = 2$, people need not continue to sanction themselves with guilt to reach a compliance equilibrium. To not feel guilt can minimize their cost of compliance and can effect an increase in their net utility.

To illustrate, suppose a health norm entrepreneur introduces a non-smoking norm for pregnant women at time $t = 0$. At time $t = 1$, a pregnant woman may choose to comply or not comply, where her utility is a function of normative claims and the age of the norm. Both first- and second-party enforcement are present during this period. She may feel guilty, or her family members may disapprove, but nonetheless she is able to weigh the two behavioral options. As the norm approaches time $t = 2$, the norm entrepreneur, and other social relations, begin to rely more on the other enforcement that has been set in motion. The utility that she assigns to compliance, independent of the norm entrepreneur's validity claims, e.g. the medical evidence, may have increased because the norm is now more traditional. At the beginning of the second period, costly normative investment and second-party enforcement stop, while the same level of utility for compliance remains. While disapproval or approval utility have decreased to nothing, the difference has been made up by increases in other sources of utility from obedience to tradition, or other forms of intrapersonal enforcement.

This logic remains as she approaches time $t = 3$. First-party enforcement is costly for her. If she remembers that she once considered smoking during pregnancy as an option, she receives disutility. The very fact that she once considered behavior outside of an established norm produces guilt. Instead, she eliminates that disutility by forgetting her past contemplation. At the beginning of the third period, she has forgotten the noncompliant behavior.[21]

While this example describes the disappearance of first-party enforcement within a personal lifetime, a general theory of subconscious social norms allows for any number of persons and any length of time between periods. Suppose each person is drawn from a single large population to play a symmetric compliance game. Each person is associated with a pure strategy: they can either play comply and remember, or comply and forget. Compliance is assured, but payoffs potentially include first- and second-party enforcement. When two persons playing *comply and remember* are matched, they pay an intrapersonal guilt cost because they are reminded that they once considered (or indeed, played) a noncompliant strategy. However, they receive a second-party approval benefit: each approves of the other's compliant behavior in the shadow of a previous wrong. When two agents play *comply and forget*, they each receive a benefit for alleviating their guilty consciences, but receive no extra approval benefit because noncompliance is not compared. When one strategy is played against the other, the agent playing *remember* pays a guilt cost, and the agent playing *forget* pays a disapproval cost for their lack of guilty conscience, yet she does not know why. She has no ability to know because she has forgotten (or has never known) that

[21] Pride can work in the same way. As soon as the compliance equilibrium is established at time $t = 2$, the magnitude of utility for a pride benefit begins to diminish with a person's memory of the noncompliance option. This is especially the case for people who are averse to pride benefits.

	Comply and remember	*Comply and forget*
Comply and remember	(0,0)	−1,−1
Comply and forget	−1,−1	(1,1)

Figure 3.4 Coordinated guilt elimination

noncompliance was a strategy. This may be especially the case when the two players matched vary in aspects such as age or culture. The complying agent can remind her, but such expression is costly, and tends to decrease over time as other sources of enforcement increase.

There are two Nash equilibria in pure strategies in addition to a mixed strategy equilibrium, where a player plays *remember* two-thirds of the time and *forget* one-third of the time. This game is a straightforward problem of coordination. If the players can sign a binding agreement before play, the Nash bargaining solution is (*forget*, *forget*). That profile gives the only payoff pair that is individually rational and Pareto efficient, and hence it is the only result that lies within the bargaining set.[22] In the absence of a binding agreement, following Harsanyi and Selten, (*forget*, *forget*) may be classified as a focal point because it payoff-dominates the strategy profile (*remember*, *remember*).[23] In short, elimination of intrapersonal sanctioning is not certain, but it is possible. In the shadow of normative investment, a pre-play negotiation, or a Pareto-dominated focal point will lead to compliance without any sort of pride, guilt, approval, or disapproval calculus.

3.4 CONCLUSION

This chapter asks why legislators demand costly permanent legislation when less costly temporary legislation provides the same

[22] It is individually rational because it assigns each player a utility that is at least as large as a player can guarantee for herself in the absence of an agreement, and Pareto efficient because there is no other payoff that all players like at least as much as (*forget*, *forget*): Binmore (1992).

[23] Harsanyi and Selten (1988: 355–6). See also Fon and Parisi (2008), which in order to examine choice under stochastic ignorance, assumes that cooperative norms operate as effective constraints on behavior.

benefit throughout their lifetime. That question led us to consider the benefit of leaving a normative legacy. Legislators who act as norm entrepreneurs can benefit from legislation that embodies their desired norm. Elsewhere, legal expression has implied an expression of the law, or of the state. This chapter emphasizes the human agency of legal expression. The law or the state are understood to reflect the normative desires of legislators or the groups that they represent. Supposing that two laws provide the substantively same legislation, but one governs permanently and the other temporarily, the permanent law can be more costly in the short to medium term. This was shown to be the case when permanent legislation governs perpetually without repeal, and when the future period costs of temporary legislation are decreasing because of legal expression.

Yet legislators who choose to legislate permanently will not realize the perpetual benefits of permanent legislation if they are approaching retirement, nor will they realize the transactions cost savings by temporarily legislating irrespective of their tenures. One possibility for why they may incur the additional cost of permanent legislation is that they receive the benefit of increasing the likelihood of leaving a normative legacy. In the long term, social norms can exist independently of first- and second-party compliance and induce involuntary compliance. The benefit from creating these norms can be reflected in the portion of benefits not realized within the lifetime of the legislator or the forgone savings offered by a temporary timing rule. Instead of legislating temporarily in order to avoid paying for the benefits that flow beyond their tenure or realize the cost savings during their tenure, legislators incur the additional costs in order to create a long-term normative legacy. Given reelection, younger legislators have more opportunities to legislate and leave a legacy while older legislators nearing retirement have fewer. This implies that older legislators demand higher levels of permanent legislation than younger legislators. This theory will be tested in chapter 6.

4. Information and commitment

4.1 INTRODUCTION

In the previous chapters we examined the use of temporary legislation during strategic interaction between the legislature and citizens. We now turn to the use of temporary legislation between the legislature and interest groups. While the public can be considered an interest group, the distinction we draw by definition is that citizen behavior is malleable through residual effects like legal expression, while interest group behavior is not. Interest group behavior can certainly reflect normative updates due to an expressive effect, but this chapter focuses on the strategic problem when their behavior is fixed and independent of those effects.[1]

The interaction we examine falls under the general heading of asymmetric information. Interest groups or their lobbies possess information that may influence a legislative outcome, and they must decide whether or not to reveal it. This problem has been studied extensively,[2] but the option to legislate temporarily or permanently is a nuance that has received little attention. The literature on statutory timing rules generally claims that temporary legislation enhances social welfare in uncertain legislative environments because temporary legislation optimally incorporates new information into the legislative process (Parisi et al. 2004, Gersen 2007, Gersen and Posner 2007, Luppi and Parisi 2009). Unlike permanent legisla-

---

[1] The model applies to any group whose behavior is independent of residual effects, though we refer to an interest group throughout the chapter for exposition. We sometimes use lobby as an interchangeable term. Lobbies are understood to represent interest groups and therefore can hold private information on behalf of interest groups. Thus lobbies can reveal or not reveal as agents of their interest group principals. Throughout, we assume no agency costs, that is, lobbies perfectly represent their principals' preferences.

[2] See Grossman and Helpman (2001).

tion, temporary legislation guarantees repeated interactions with a lobby by default, which are thought to incentivize the lobby to make honest claims (Lohmann 1995). For example, Gersen (2007) provides a case study of the Terrorism Risk Insurance Act of 2002 which was enacted with a three-year sunset.[3] Congress was uncertain of the scope of the new terrorism risk and of the consequent need for new legislation. Given the uncertainty, temporary legislation was expected to enhance welfare by enabling the revelation of information by the insurance industry. Of primary concern was whether or not private insurance markets could provide coverage without government backstop.[4] A temporary timing rule guaranteed repeated interactions with the relevant lobby (The Coalition to Insure Against Terrorism) since the law was configured to expire in three years. Thus if the insurance industry could or could not provide insurance on its own, that fact might be expected to surface in hearing at the three-year sunset. Nonetheless, the issue was not emphasized, though in 2005 Congress extended the legislation with higher triggers.[5]

This example points to the central question of this chapter. Under what conditions does temporary legislation guarantee information revelation? Clearly, a legislature can simply pass a law temporarily in an attempt to procure information, only to let it expire if that attempt fails. Moreover, lobbies (or their interest group principals) may sacrifice potential reputation benefits from fully revealing their knowledge in order to maintain a favorable legal environment. Two necessary conditions for a revealing equilibrium under temporary legislation, then, are that the legislature must be committed to the issue and that interest groups must have something to gain by revealing, or lose by not revealing.

Information asymmetry dominates the contemporary study of regulation. Regulators require information to determine the existence of market failure due to concentrated market power, externalities, or lack of information regarding product hazards. In each case,

---

[3] Terrorism Risk Insurance Act of 2002, Pub. L. No. 107-297, Stat. 2322 (2002).

[4] This was not a new concern. The insurance industry has lobbied Congress for a backstop on other occasions for reasons unrelated to terrorism (Gersen 2007: 296–7).

[5] Terrorism Risk Insurance Extension Act of 2005, Pub. L. No. 109-144, 119 Stat. 2660 (2005).

regulators require information to identify the market failure and to determine the optimal regulatory response. Likewise, information asymmetry dominates the principal–agent theory that guides many of the conclusions of the study of bureaucratic decisionmaking. Principal–agent relationships take the form of executive–regulator, legislature–regulator, and courts–regulator. In each case, the government branch attempts to procure information from the regulator in order to identify regulatory failure and to provide an additional level of oversight (Posner, E. A. 2001, Stephenson 2008). While much of the literature focuses on the regulator–firm and legislature–regulator relationships, our model explicitly deals with the direct relationship between the legislature and the interest group or lobby as in Grossman and Helpman (2001), Lohmann (1995), Rasmusen (1993), and in the literature on statutory timing rules mentioned above.

The legislature's need for information

Coglianese et al. (2004) identifies four general areas where the legislature requires information in order to create socially optimal rules. For laws that address externalities or lack of disclosure regarding product hazards, the legislature requires information on the *magnitude and probability* of the harm that a legislative issue is producing. Understanding of magnitude and probability permits lawmakers to optimally set penalties. Legislatures also need to discern the *cause* of the issue. Understanding of the cause of harm helps legislatures to avoid the errors of prohibiting behavior that produces no harm at all and leaving the behavior that produces harm unaddressed. Third, legislation, especially regulatory rules, typically specifies the behavior that firms or individuals may not practice. Thus, the legislature needs to know the various behavioral *options* that are available in place of a prohibited action. Lastly, information regarding the *consequences* of legislation is needed. This information includes the cost of compliance, to what extent compliance will deliver social benefits, how it will impact innovation, and whether or not the legislation will produce unintended effects.

Legislatures have five ways to procure this information. First, it is well established that the American legislature and courts can request information under threat of penalty.[6] Yet this technique suffers

---

[6] McGrain v. Daugherty, 273 U.S. 135 (1927), and see Landis (1926).

from two shortcomings. Legislatures must already possess enough information in order to know what to ask, and legislatures may not be able to determine if they receive a complete answer.[7] Second, legislatures can request information without threat of penalty. Non-mandatory requests can take the form of public hearings, advisory committees, etc. Presumably, lobbies will only reveal information that will produce a private net benefit for revelation, leaving potentially useful information undisclosed. Third, legislatures can request information in exchange for a benefit. This is generally seen with patent protection, drug approval, safety standards licensing, and other explicit benefits granted for participation in legislative pilot projects. Fourth, legislatures can rely on informal interaction with lobbies. Contemporary study of informational strategy for policy making suggests that informal interaction is important, especially in light of the difficulties associated with mandatory and non-mandatory information requests. Unlike formal interaction, informal interaction can overcome collective silence throughout a policy domain because legislators can secretly reward single firms or individuals for breaking the silence, preserving the informer's deniability. This line of reasoning produces two conclusions that run counter to prevailing economic theory: opacity can enhance welfare and regulatory capture can enhance welfare since capture may entail closer relationships which promote informal interaction (Coglianese et al. 2004: 341). Lastly, legislatures can procure information by legislating, if legislating changes behavior and reveals information in the process.

New legislation can reveal each of the four general types of information (magnitude, cause, options, and consequences) by deducing information from the differences between pre- and post-legislative environments. The following examples are crude, and are meant to demonstrate the logic of post-legislative deduction.

Consider first an unknown magnitude of harm. Table 4.1 shows how new legislation may reveal that information, given that the legislature can observe the total harm before the enactment.

---

[7] Coglianese et al. (2004: 311) gives an example where the American Environmental Protection Agency created an amnesty program waiving penalties for firms that disclosed studies on toxins. The amnesty program produced 11,000 studies that Congress did not ask for explicitly prior to the implementation of the program.

Table 4.1 Legislating the revelation of harm magnitude

	State 1	State 2	Deduction
Total harm	100	50	–
Interest group harm	x	0	50%
Non-interest group harm	y	50	50%
Legislation	none	targets interest group	–

Table 4.2 Legislating the revelation of harm cause

	State 1	State 2	Deduction
Outcome	x	−x	–
Possible cause 1	unknown	not occurring	true
Possible cause 2	unknown	occurring	false
Legislation	none	prohibit cause 1	–

In state 1, the legislature observes a total harm of 100 and knows that a particular interest group is a contributor, but not fully responsible. In state 2, it observes a total harm of 50 in a legislative environment that prohibits the lobby from contributing. The deduction that the lobby is producing 50 percent of the harm follows.

Information regarding an unknown cause can be similarly deduced. The legislature observes outcome x prior to legislating, and considers two possible causes. Prohibiting possible cause 1 and not observing outcome x, leads to the deduction that possible cause 1 yields outcome x: see Table 4.2.

Comparing pre- and post-legislative environments can reveal available behavioral options as well. For example, in the 1970s regulators were uncertain if completely banning chlorofluorocarbon (CFC) propellants was feasible because they were uncertain of the economic viability of a substitute propellant. Before new regulation was introduced, S. C. Johnson Wax Company eliminated all CFC propellants from its products and began to rely exclusively on the water-based propellants that it had developed twenty years earlier. Their decision, which rested upon the fact that the complete substitution of water-based propellants was economically viable, revealed the feasibility of a complete ban on CFC propellants. Likewise, a legislative ban prior to S. C. Johnson's decision may have revealed

Table 4.3 Legislating the revelation of behavioral options

	State 1	State 2	Deduction
Outcome	observed	observed	–
Option 1	observed	unobserved	–
Option 2	unobserved	observed	feasible
Legislation	none	prohibits option 1	–

their ability to substitute water-based alternatives. An effective ban, where noncompliance was sufficiently costly, would have led S. C. Johnson to begin a full substitution of its water-based propellants. Generally, if the legislature is aware of two possible options, yet prohibits one and observes the same outcome, then the feasibility of the other option is revealed: see Table 4.3.

Finally, the legislature can deduce the consequences of legislation. This is straightforward. The cost of compliance, to what extent compliance will deliver social benefits, how it will impact innovation, and whether or not the legislation will produce unintended effects are all more easily observed after the legislation has been enacted. Of course that information is particularly valuable prior to enactment, but in some cases it may not be possible to obtain.

All of the preceding examples regarding how legislation can reveal information pertaining to magnitude, cause, options, and consequences are meant to demonstrate that legislating is a further method available to the legislature for procuring information in addition to mandatory and non-mandatory disclosure, exchange, or informal interaction. Legislation can indirectly reveal information through precipitating an adjustment in behavior. However, a timing rule may impact its ability to do so.

At first glance, it may seem that permanent legislation may send a stronger signal regarding the legislators' commitment to the policy and consequently induce adjustments in behavior to a greater extent than temporary legislation. Interest groups may believe that a permanent enactment may be more costly to legislators than a temporary enactment, and that the legislators' insistence on incurring higher enactment costs may signal their intention to not repeal. Partial or no compliance with permanent legislation, especially when its repeal is unexpected, may be sufficiently costly to the interest group, and the high expected costs of compliance may induce an adjustment in behavior that reveals information. On the other hand, temporary legislation may send a signal of weak commitment, and if its expiration is expected, it may not be sufficiently costly to induce an adjustment. Interest groups who anticipate the expiration of temporary legislation may conceal information regarding magnitude, cause, and available behavioral options. Information can be concealed through temporary noncompliance. Likewise, information can be concealed through effecting compliance only in the short term. For example, firms can simply refrain from the prohibited behavior temporarily, making no capital investment required for compliance, and resume their behavior when the prohibition expires. While this type of "wait-it-out" behavior may reveal information regarding magnitude and cause under some circumstances, it always conceals information regarding available behavioral options.

In spite of the "wait-it-out" strategy available to interest groups, a temporary enactment can precipitate an adjustment in behavior. In the previous chapters, we have shown that permanent and temporary legislation can govern for more, less, or equal lengths of time through legislative maintenance. Moreover, expectations of commitment are not exclusively based upon the timing rule since repeals, amendments, and extensions are further tied to a dynamic legislative environment. Expectations of political turnover, changing tastes, new technology, among others, all play a role. Our model specifies the conditions for temporary legislation to indirectly reveal information through an adjustment in interest group behavior in spite of these possibilities.

Perhaps more importantly, temporary legislation guarantees repeated interaction with the interest group's representative lobby regarding a specific policy. The prospect of repeated interaction may reveal information directly, irrespective of how an interest group adjusts its behavior around a new law, and we will examine under what conditions information will be revealed in this manner as well.

4.2 THE MODEL

A single lobby and a controlling group of legislators are two players in a game that takes place over one period. There are three states of the world $R \in \{\rho_1, \rho_2, \rho_3\}$, which describe the legislators' preferences for commitment to the legislation and alignment with the lobby, i.e.

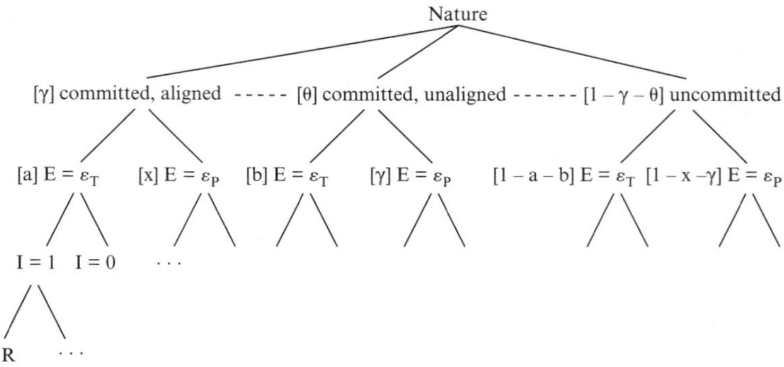

Figure 4.1 Stylized model of information revelation given a temporary or permanent enactment

committed, aligned; committed, unaligned; and uncommitted. At the beginning of the game, nature chooses the true state, which the lobby does not observe. Legislators move second to choose $E \in \{\varepsilon_T, \varepsilon_P\}$, the binary decision between enacting a temporary timing rule (ε_T) and enacting a permanent timing rule (ε_P). Contingent upon the observed timing rule, the lobby moves to choose $I \in \{1,0\}$, the binary decision between revealing or not revealing information. Finally, the legislators follow up their initial enactment by choosing $\hat{R}$ to equal ρ_1 (committed, aligned), ρ_2 (committed, unaligned), or ρ_3 (uncommitted).

The order of play can be summarized as:

1. Nature chooses the legislative environment R to equal ρ_1 (committed, aligned) with probability γ, ρ_2 (committed, unaligned) with probability θ, or ρ_3 (uncommitted) with probability $1 - \gamma - \theta$.
2. Legislators choose the enactment timing rule E, where (ε_T) indicates a temporary timing rule and (ε_P) indicates a permanent timing rule.
3. The lobby chooses I to equal 1 (reveal information) or 0 (do not reveal information).
4. Legislators choose $\hat{R}$ to equal ρ_1, ρ_2 or ρ_3.

As in chapter 2, the legislators' payoff is dependent on enactment and maintenance costs. Maintenance costs m are incurred whenever the legislature extends temporary legislation, and repeals or amends permanent legislation. Thus a group of legislators who are committed to a policy, i.e. $(\gamma + \theta) = 1$, will incur extension costs if they enact that policy with a temporary timing rule as indicated by the second term. Uncommitted legislators are understood to let the temporary enactment expire and do not incur those costs:

$$\pi_l = \hat{R} - m[\varepsilon_T(\gamma + \theta) + \varepsilon_P I(\gamma + \theta)] - E[\varepsilon_P I(\gamma + \theta)] - E \qquad (4.1)$$

The second term also accounts for the repeal costs incurred by a group of legislators who legislate permanently and later repeal or amend that legislation in order to adapt it to the information revealed by the lobby. The third term accounts for the cost of the adapted enactment. The last term E represents the cost of sending the signal, which is also the initial enactment cost. Finally, the legislators receive the policy benefit given by $\hat{R}$.

The lobby payoff accounts for the cost of the new legislation, which can be understood as a compliance cost, as well as two additional components unique to the strategic interaction surrounding temporary timing rules:

$$\pi_\lambda = -\hat{R} + aI(\gamma - \theta) + rI(\gamma + \theta) \qquad (4.2)$$

First, if the lobby is in state of the world ρ_1 $(\gamma = 1)$, its interests are aligned with those of the legislators and any adjustment to the legislation based upon the information that they reveal increases its payoff by a. Instead, if the lobby is in state of the world ρ_2 $(\theta = 1)$, its interests are not aligned and any adjustment based upon revealed information decreases its payoff by a. Second, revealing information to committed legislators, irrespective of alignment, increases lobby payoff with reputation utility r, while revealing information to uncommitted legislators yields no increase.

The legislators and the lobby know all of the values of the parameters ρ, β, m, ε_T, ε_P, a, and r. ρ represents the policy benefit to the legislators and its symmetrical policy cost to the lobby; m, ε_T and ε_P are the value of the maintenance and enactment costs; a and r are the values of policy adjustment and lobby reputation. Lastly, we assume that given no maintenance, the value of a permanent enactment is greater than the value of a temporary enactment since a permanent enactment with no repeal provides an infinite stream of benefits and a temporary enactment with no extension provides a finite stream of benefits. This is notated by subscripting policy benefits ρ with P and T when $m = 0$.

The equilibrium payoffs will be derived for three different settings which are distinguished for their relationship between the adjustment and reputation values. We will examine the settings where $a > r$, $r > a$, and $a = r$.

4.3 EQUILIBRIUM ANALYSIS

A strategy profile of the temporary timing rule game is represented by the ordered nontuple $(X, Y, Z; L, R; f, g; x, y)$, where

X = legislators' action if committed, aligned
Y = legislators' action if committed, unaligned
Z = legislators' action if uncommitted
L = lobby's action if ε_T is observed
R = lobby's action if ε_P is observed
f = lobby's belief, given ε_T, that legislators are committed, aligned
g = lobby's belief, given ε_T, that legislators are committed, unaligned
x = lobby's belief, given ε_P, that legislators are committed, aligned
y = lobby's belief, given ε_P, that legislators are committed, unaligned

4.3.1 The Insufficient Reputation Reward Setting

When the value of adjustment exceeds the value of reputation, the temporary timing rule game yields a single perfect Bayesian equilibrium $(\varepsilon_T, \varepsilon_P, \varepsilon_P; 1, 0; \frac{\gamma}{\gamma+\theta}, \frac{\theta}{\gamma+\theta}, \gamma, \theta)$.[8] The lobby reveals information under a temporary timing rule, but only because it believes that its interests are aligned with the legislators' interests.[9] As the probability that the legislators are {committed, aligned} (γ) increases, we see that $f = \frac{\gamma}{\gamma+\theta}$, which is the lobby's probabilistic belief that legislators are {committed, aligned}, approaches 1.

Similarly, as the probability that legislators are {committed,

[8] Proofs are given in the chapter appendix.

[9] Let $\gamma = 1$. The lobby payoff for revealing is $\pi_\lambda^{I=1} = -\hat{R} - a + r$, which is greater than the lobby payoff for not revealing given by $\pi_\lambda^{I=0} = -\hat{R}$. If $\theta = 1$, the lobby payoff for revealing is $\pi_\lambda^{I=1} = -\hat{R} - a + r$, which is less than the lobby payoff for not revealing given by $\pi_\lambda^{I=0} = -\hat{R}$ since $a > r$.

unaligned} (θ) decreases, f approaches 1. The lobby is never entirely certain, however, and will not reveal in the ρ_2 state in order to avoid incurring possible adjustment costs. Thus, when $a > r$ the only possibility for information revelation following a temporary enactment is when legislator and lobby interests are aligned. This equilibrium holds irrespective of the existence of reputation benefits, and emphasizes their insufficiency to reveal complete or truthful information when adjustment costs are too great.

Insufficient reputation rewards may partly explain why the necessity of a government backstop for terrorism insurance was scarcely mentioned during the Terrorism Risk Insurance Act hearings. Congress was committed to providing a legislative response, but could not provide a backstop if it could be shown that the insurance market could function on its own. The members of The Coalition to Insure Against Terrorism may have gained reputation benefits from revealing additional information regarding their ability or inability to provide insurance, but those benefits may have been outweighed by the adjustment cost of a possible elimination or reduction of the backstop.

4.3.2 The Sufficient Reputation Reward Setting

When $r > a$, the temporary timing rule game yields two perfect Bayesian equilibria $(\varepsilon_T, \varepsilon_T, \varepsilon_P; 1, 1; \gamma, \theta, 0, 0)$ and $(\varepsilon_T, \varepsilon_T, \varepsilon_P; 1, 0; \frac{\gamma}{\gamma + \theta}, \frac{\theta}{\gamma + \theta}, 0, 0)$. In both equilibria, the lobby always reveals information under a temporary enactment even when legislators and lobby interests are unaligned ($\theta = 1$). This is because the payoff for revealing exceeds the payoff for not revealing when the reputation value exceeds the adjustment value in both the ρ_1 and ρ_2 states.[10]

In section 4.1, we questioned temporary legislation's ability to credibly signal a long-term legislative commitment, and now address this question with the following lemma.

Lemma 5 *When the reputation value exceeds the adjustment value, the lobby knows with certainty that legislators who send a temporary enactment signal are committed to the policy.*

---

[10] When $\gamma = 1$ or $\theta = 1$, the lobby payoff for revealing is $\pi_\lambda^{I=1} = -\hat{R} - a + r$, which is greater than the lobby payoff for not revealing given by $\pi_\lambda^{1=0} = -\hat{R}$ since $r > a$.

Proof. When $r > a$ there are two perfect Bayesian equilibria $(\varepsilon_T, \varepsilon_T, \varepsilon_P; 1, 1; \gamma, \theta, 0, 0)$ and $(\varepsilon_T, \varepsilon_T, \varepsilon_P; 1, 0; \frac{\gamma}{\gamma + \theta}, \frac{\theta}{\gamma + \theta}, 0, 0)$. It is straightforward that only committed legislators send temporary signals and uncommitted legislators send permanent signals. □

This result demonstrates that a temporary enactment can actually signal commitment to a long-term policy in spite of the fact that legislators legislate temporarily instead of permanently. This is because adapting permanent legislation to revealed information is more costly than adapting temporary legislation to revealed information. Adaption of permanent legislation requires placing the item on the legislative agenda, along with amendment or repeal, while adaption of temporary legislation requires only a new enactment since expiration places the item on the legislative agenda by default. Since committed legislators know that the lobby will reveal information in exchange for reputation benefits, their signal to legislate temporarily demonstrates that they are optimizing around adapting the legislation to the revealed information. Uncommitted legislators do not incur adaption costs and thus optimize by legislating permanently. It is for this reason that the committed and uncommitted types separate when the enactment signal is sent.

4.3.3 The Equivalence Setting

When $r = a$, each of the three perfect Bayesian equilibria discussed above obtain. While $(\varepsilon_T, \varepsilon_T, \varepsilon_P; 1, 1; \gamma, \theta, 0, 0)$ and $(\varepsilon_T, \varepsilon_T, \varepsilon_P; 1, 0; \frac{\gamma}{\gamma + \theta}, \frac{\theta}{\gamma + \theta}, 0, 0)$ lead to the separation of committed and uncommitted legislators for a given enactment, the signal is disturbed by the addition of $(\varepsilon_T, \varepsilon_P, \varepsilon_P; 1, 0; \frac{\gamma}{\gamma + \theta}, \frac{\theta}{\gamma + \theta}, \gamma, \theta)$. The third equilibrium does not survive a Pareto dominance refinement since strategies and payoffs are identical in ρ_1, the adjustment and reputation values for revealing information following a temporary enactment cancel out in ρ_2,[11] and the payoffs for revealing or not revealing to uncommitted legislators are identical. While we include the equivalence setting for the sake of completeness, we think that the two

---

[11] The cancellation means that the payoff for revealing information equals the payoff for not revealing information. Let $\theta = 1$. When $r = a$, $\pi_\lambda^{I=1} = -\hat{R} = a(\gamma - \theta) = rI(\gamma + \theta) = -\hat{R} = \pi_\lambda^{I=0}$.

settings where $a > r$ and $r > a$ deserve the most attention. In section 4.2 the simplifying assumption that a and r are perfectly known was made, though it is probably more likely that their relative values are better known than their precise values. Legislators and lobbies may not know the precise value of a reputation benefit or adjustment cost, but they may have a better idea that an adjustment is more costly than a gain in reputation or that a gain in reputation is more beneficial than an adjustment.

4.4 COMPARING WELFARE

Table 4.4 summarizes the comparative statics for the payoffs, where (+) indicates variables that increase payoffs and (−) indicates variables that decrease payoffs. The legislators' payoff, given in equation 4.1, is increasing in the policy benefit ρ. It is decreasing in enactment and maintenance costs, and it is decreasing in commitment, (γ) and (θ). Commitment decreases their payoff indirectly in that it leads to further maintenance.

The lobby's payoff, given in equation 4.2, is decreasing in the policy cost ρ and is independent of enactment and maintenance. It is increasing in commitment, alignment (γ) because both adjustment and reputation utility is marginally increased when information is revealed. It is decreasing in the product of commitment, unalignment and adjustment ($a\theta$) and increasing in the product of commitment, unalignment and reputation ($r\theta$) because unaligned legislators use revealed information to follow up with a more costly policy, but confer reputation benefits.

Proposition 6 *Permanent timing rules raise welfare when legislators are less committed, legislative maintenance costs are higher, and the lobby valuation of adjustment and reputation is lower, i.e.* γ, θ, *a and r are small, and m is large.*

Table 4.4 Comparative statics

	γ	$a\theta$	$r\theta$	ρ	m	ε_T	ε_p
π_l	−	−	−	+	−	−	−
π_λ	+	−	+	−	0	0	0

Proposition 6 suggests that the use of permanent timing rules should be encouraged when legislators are less committed to refining a policy to ideally suit a legislative environment since the cost of doing so with temporary timing rules is realized through numerous temporary enactments. Each of these enactments offers legislators the opportunity to adjust the policy to the environment, but each enactment is costly.[12] If legislators are less committed to refining the policy and consequently make few policy adaptions, the costs of numerous temporary enactments can be avoided with a permanent timing rule.

Small adjustment and reputation values for the lobby follow the same line of reasoning. When lobbies consider the value of a beneficial adjustment to a policy and an enhanced reputation to be sufficiently low, their adjustment and reputation benefit is outweighed by the costs of multiple temporary enactments. A permanent timing rule in this circumstance enhances welfare because it allows legislators to legislate once without expiration. A permanent timing rule forgoes the benefit of adjustment, but it avoids the cost of the multiple temporary enactments. While the model allows for the adjustment of permanent legislation through repeal and new enactment or amendment, those costs are outweighed by sufficiently low adjustment and reputation benefits in the same manner that the costs of multiple temporary enactments are outweighed by sufficiently low adjustment and reputation benefits.

Less-committed legislators and low-value adjustments point to a use of permanent timing rules when the precision of legal rules is not valued by both parties. Ehrlich and Posner (1974), comparing statutory with judge-made law, conclude that statutory law should be encouraged when legal precision is highly valued. This is because they understand statutes to be less ambiguous than judge-made law. Our result that permanent timing rules should be encouraged when adjustments are less valued runs somewhat counter to their conclusion.

The key to proposition 6 however is the low adjustment benefit. A permanent statute governs in perpetuity by default and avoids the cost of repeatedly placing legislation on the agenda that offers little adjustment benefit. A temporary statute expires automatically, and

---

[12] See chapter 2, section 2.2.3.

requires further action if it is to govern beyond its expiration. This is unlike judge-made law, which requires further action only if a case is brought to trial. Only then may the law be adjusted and costs incurred. It is the additional enactment costs of temporary legislation which lead us to conclude that permanent legislation should be encouraged when adjustment is not particularly valued. It may be that adjustment is not valued at all if the legislation is understood to be already precise at the time of enactment and to require no further adaption in a future period. *Ex ante* precision, i.e., $a = 0$ or sufficiently small a, is a qualification to the conclusion given in Ehrlich and Posner (1974) that statutes should be encouraged when precision is highly valued.

High maintenance costs also favor permanent timing rules. Each time a temporary enactment expires, new legislation must be enacted according to constitutional rules. In chapter 2, we divide maintenance costs into variable and fixed components. The variable component represents the cost of satisfying the preferences of interest groups, including the public. The fixed component represents the cost of adhering to the constitutional rules of bicameralism and presentment. These costs are incurred each time a temporary enactment expires and is extended or replaced by new legislation. If these costs outweigh the benefit of adjustment, permanent timing rules may raise welfare. While our model describes a controlling group of legislators with homogeneous preferences, accounting for heterogeneous preferences within the legislature reinforces the result. A coalition that will lose control may attempt to use a permanent timing rule in order to legislate beyond their mandate. If the new majority highly values an adjustment, they will incur repeal or amendment costs which include placement onto the legislative agenda. Those costs could have otherwise been avoided with a temporary timing rule.

Proposition 7 *Temporary timing rules raise welfare when legislators are more committed, legislative maintenance costs are lower, the value of reputation is higher, and the value of adjustment is lower when legislator and lobby interests are unaligned, i.e. when* γ *and* r *are large, and* $a\theta$ *and* m *are small.*

Proposition 7 suggests that the use of temporary timing rules should be encouraged when legislators are more committed to refining a policy to ideally suit a legislative environment since the automatic expiration of temporary enactments avoids numerous repeals or amendments of permanent enactments and placements of the issue onto the legislative agenda. However, committed legislators need information in order to adapt the policy to the legislative environment. As shown in the equilibrium analysis, lobbies reveal information to committed legislators under temporary timing rules when legislator and lobby interests are aligned. When lobbies reveal information, committed legislators are able to adapt the policy without paying additional repeal or amendment costs. Lobbies benefit from the policy adjustment and the reputation benefit. Thus temporary timing rules enhance welfare when γ is large.

The equilibrium analysis has also shown that lobbies reveal information to committed legislators when legislator and lobby interests are not aligned. In this setting, revealing information increases the lobby reputation at the expense of a tougher policy. Only if reputation benefits exceed adjustment costs, will the lobby reveal information. As when interests are aligned, revealed information permits committed legislators to adapt the policy without paying additional repeal or amendment costs. Lobbies benefit from a sufficient increase in reputation even though they pay an adjustment cost. Thus temporary timing rules enhance welfare when r is large, and $a\theta$ is small.

Low maintenance costs also favor temporary timing rules. Each time temporary legislation is extended or replaced by new legislation, legislators incur variable and fixed maintenance costs. When these costs are sufficiently low, they are outweighed by the benefits offered by temporary timing rules: adjustment and reputation benefits under committed and aligned legislators, or sufficient reputation benefits under committed and unaligned legislators. Permanent timing rules avoid the maintenance costs, but do not offer the adjustment and reputation benefits available under temporary timing rules. Thus temporary timing rules enhance welfare when m is small.

4.5 CONCLUSION

Legislators require information in order to address social welfare optimally. In some cases, lobbies have useful information, but do not have sufficient incentive to reveal it. Legislators have five ways to procure that information. They can make mandatory requests, they can make non-mandatory requests, they can offer a publicly viewed benefit like a patent or a license in exchange, they can offer a privately viewed benefit through informal interaction with a lobby, or they can legislate. Legislation can incentivize lobbies to reveal information indirectly through observable changes in compliance behavior, or directly through repeated interaction with legislators. The latter occurs by default when legislators use a temporary timing rule because expiration and a potential reenactment is guaranteed. When the lobby values reputation less than adjustment, information is revealed following a temporary enactment only to committed and aligned legislators. This is because aligned legislators use the revealed information to adjust the legislation in the lobby's favor. When the lobby values reputation more than adjustment, information is revealed following a temporary enactment to committed legislators, irrespective of their alignment. This result implies that when reputation exceeds adjustment, a temporary enactment signals a legislative commitment and a permanent enactment does not. This is because committed legislators adjust legislation, and adjusting a temporary enactment is less costly than adjusting a permanent enactment.

It normatively follows that committed and unaligned legislators should increase reputation benefits in order to give the lobby incentive to reveal. Committed legislators adjust legislation to optimally address social welfare as they receive more information regarding the legislative environment. Yet because their interests are unaligned with lobby interests, the lobby does not reveal information that provides a basis for adjustment. The status quo information level suboptimally addresses social welfare, and is maintained with permanent legislation or no legislation. Instead, committed and unaligned legislators who increase reputation benefits can induce the lobby to reveal information, which provides a basis for a socially optimal adjustment. In this case, legislators should select a temporary timing rule in order to minimize transactions cost.

APPENDIX

Equilibria proofs. Consider the profile $(\varepsilon_T, \varepsilon_P, \varepsilon_P; 1, 0; \frac{\gamma}{\gamma+\theta}, \frac{\theta}{\gamma+\theta}, \gamma, \theta)$ when $a > r$. We first verify the legislators' signaling strategy given the lobby's information strategy. Recall that the legislators' payoff is $\pi_l = \hat{R} - m[\varepsilon_T(\gamma+\theta) + \varepsilon_P I(\gamma+\theta)] - E[\varepsilon_P I(\gamma+\theta)] - E$. Committed and aligned legislators send a temporary enactment signal because $\rho - m\varepsilon_T - E > \rho - m\varepsilon_P - E(\varepsilon_P - 1)$. Committed and unaligned legislators send a permanent enactment signal because $\rho - E > \rho - m\varepsilon_T - E$. Uncommitted legislators provide no maintenance and send a permanent enactment signal because $\rho_P - E > \rho_T - E$. We second verify the lobby's information strategy given the legislators' type-contingent strategies. Recall that the lobby payoff is $\pi_\lambda = -\hat{R} + aI(\gamma - \theta) + rI(\gamma + \theta)$. The lobby reveals information when committed and aligned legislators send a temporary signal because $-\rho + a + r > -\rho$. The lobby does not reveal information when committed and unaligned legislators send a permanent signal because $-\rho > -\rho - a + r$ and $a > r$. Likewise, the lobby does not reveal information when uncommitted legislators send a permanent signal because $-\rho = -\rho$ and $I = 0$ for all other ε_P. Lastly, we verify that given the legislators' enactment signal, any change in the lobby's posterior beliefs regarding the legislators' type is not sufficient to change the lobby's information strategy I. Since $a = p(\gamma|\varepsilon_T) = \frac{\gamma \cdot 1}{\gamma \cdot 1 + \theta \cdot 1 + (1 - r - \theta) \cdot 0} = \frac{\gamma}{\gamma + \theta}$, $b = p(\theta|\varepsilon_T) = \frac{\theta \cdot 1}{\gamma \cdot 1 + \theta \cdot 1 + (1 - \gamma - \theta) \cdot 0} = \frac{\theta}{\gamma + \theta}$, $x = p(\gamma|\varepsilon_P) = \frac{\gamma \cdot 1}{\gamma \cdot 1 + \theta \cdot 1 + (1 - \gamma - \theta) \cdot 1} = \gamma$, and $y = p(\theta|\varepsilon_P) = \frac{\theta \cdot 1}{\gamma \cdot 1 + \theta \cdot 1 + (1 - \gamma - \theta) \cdot 1} = \theta$, strategy I remains unchanged. Thus $(\varepsilon_T, \varepsilon_P, \varepsilon_P; 1, 0; \frac{\gamma}{\gamma+\theta}, \frac{\theta}{\gamma+\theta}, \gamma, \theta)$ is a perfect Bayesian equilibrium when $a > r$.

Consider the profile $(\varepsilon_T, \varepsilon_T, \varepsilon_P; 1, 0; \frac{\gamma}{\gamma+\theta}, \frac{\theta}{\gamma+\theta}, 0, 0)$ when $r > a$. Committed and aligned legislators send a temporary enactment signal because $\rho - m\varepsilon_T - E > \rho - m\varepsilon_P - E(\varepsilon_P + 1)$. Committed and unaligned legislators send a temporary enactment signal because $\rho - m\varepsilon_T - E > \rho - m\varepsilon_P - E(\varepsilon_P + 1)$. Uncommitted legislators provide no maintenance and send a permanent enactment signal because $\rho_P - E > \rho_T - E$. The lobby reveals information when committed and aligned legislators send a temporary signal because $-\rho + a + r > -\rho$. Likewise, the lobby reveals information when committed and unaligned legislators send a temporary signal because $-\rho - a + r > -\rho$ and $r > a$. The lobby is indifferent to revealing information when uncommitted legislators send a temporary or permanent signal because $-\rho = -\rho$. Since $a = p(\gamma|\varepsilon_T) = \frac{\gamma \cdot 1}{\gamma \cdot 1 + \theta \cdot 1 + (1 - \gamma - \theta) \cdot 0} = \frac{\gamma}{\gamma + \theta}$, $b = p(\theta|\varepsilon_T) = \frac{\theta \cdot 1}{\gamma \cdot 1 + \theta \cdot 1 + (1 - \gamma - \theta) \cdot 0} = \frac{\theta}{\gamma + \theta}$, $x = p(\gamma|\varepsilon_P) = \frac{\gamma \cdot 0}{\gamma \cdot 0 + \theta \cdot 0 + (1 - \gamma - \theta) \cdot 1} = 0$, and $y = p(\theta|\varepsilon_P) = \frac{\theta \cdot 0}{\gamma \cdot 0 + \theta \cdot 0 + (1 - \gamma - \theta) \cdot 1} = 0$, strategy I remains unchanged. Thus $(\varepsilon_T, \varepsilon_T, \varepsilon_P; 1, 0; \frac{\gamma}{\gamma + \theta}, \frac{\theta}{\gamma + \theta}, 0, 0)$ is a perfect Bayesian equilibrium when $r > a$.

Finally, consider the profile $(\varepsilon_T, \varepsilon_T, \varepsilon_p; 1, 1; \gamma, \theta, 0, 0)$ when $r > a$. Committed and aligned legislators send a temporary enactment signal because $\rho - m\varepsilon_T - E > \rho - m\varepsilon_P - E(\varepsilon_P + 1)$. Committed and unaligned legislators send a temporary enactment signal because $\rho - m\varepsilon_T - E > \rho - m\varepsilon_P - E(\varepsilon_P + 1)$. Uncommitted legislators provide no maintenance and send a permanent enactment signal because $\rho_P - E > \rho_T - E$. The lobby reveals information when committed and aligned legislators send a temporary signal because $-\rho + a + r > -\rho$. Likewise, the lobby reveals information when committed and unaligned legislators send a temporary signal because $-\rho - a + r > -\rho$ and $r > a$. The lobby is indifferent to revealing information when uncommitted legislators send a temporary or permanent signal because $-\rho = -\rho$. Since $a = p(\gamma|\varepsilon_T) = \frac{\gamma \cdot 1}{\gamma \cdot 1 + \theta \cdot 1 + (1 - \gamma - \theta) \cdot 1} = \gamma$, $b = p(\theta|\varepsilon_T) = \frac{\theta \cdot 1}{\gamma \cdot 1 + \theta \cdot 1 + (1 - \gamma - \theta) \cdot 1} = \theta$, $x = p(\gamma|\varepsilon_P) = \frac{\gamma \cdot 0}{\gamma \cdot 0 + \theta \cdot 0 + (1 - \gamma - \theta) \cdot 1} = 0$, and $y = p(\theta|\varepsilon_P) = \frac{\theta \cdot 0}{\gamma \cdot 0 + \theta \cdot 0 + (1 - \gamma - \theta) \cdot 1} = 0$, strategy I remains unchanged. Thus $(\varepsilon_T, \varepsilon_T, \varepsilon_P; 1, 1; \gamma, \theta, 0, 0)$ is a perfect Bayesian equilibrium when $r > a$.

5. Temporary tax legislation

5.1 INTRODUCTION

While temporary fiscal policies are at least as old as the American constitution,[1] the frequency and intensity of their strategic use in the United States has sensationally increased in the past fifteen years. At the beginning of 2000, more than one hundred American tax provisions were scheduled to expire, including some of the largest tax cuts in history. Only a decade prior, less than two dozen relatively inconsequential provisions were scheduled to expire. The increase from 1990 to 2000 continued into the following decade: during fiscal year 2011, 251 tax provisions were scheduled to expire (Kysar 2011: 1010). As a result, there has been a steady output of legal scholarship on temporary taxation, which, in the main, observes that temporary timing rules promote irresponsible fiscal imbalances for three reasons. First, temporary timing rules ease the passage of spending increases and tax cuts. Because temporary tax legislation lasts for a relatively shorter time if it is not extended, it more easily satisfies current budget rules and is less opposed by opposition legislators and citizens. It therefore is more likely to become law. Second, most of the scholarship recognizes that temporary tax legislation easily circumvents budgetary rules that require offsetting, i.e. concomitant increases in taxation or reductions in outstanding spending, that are, in theory, supposed to render new spending increases or tax cuts budget neutral. Because offset rules are easily circumvented, temporary timing rules facilitate passage of spending increases or tax cuts that increase the deficit. This process will be explained in the following section. Third, temporary tax legislation is subject to

1 Article I, § 8 provides that "[t]he Congress shall have Power to lay and collect Taxes, Duties, Imposts and Excises, . . . [in order] to raise and support Armies, but no Appropriation of Money to that Use shall be for a longer Term than two Years."

inertia. Future legislatures are routinely forced to extend temporary changes or lose political power. Failure to extend a popular spending program or tax cut can be politically costly; thus, the expected budgetary cost of a temporary change is actually much greater than the initial budgetary cost used for its accounting.

Opponents of temporary taxation provide examples of temporary enactments which were extended at each expiration, and argue that the inertia of a temporary enactment typically propels it to de facto permanent status. If legislatures were required to account for the expected costs of a temporary enactment, its estimated total cost would be much greater. This is because the potential costs of each extension would necessarily be included in that estimate. When considering those costs, it would be far less likely that a temporary change to the tax code would acquire the political support for its passage, and would fail to become law as a result (Garrett 2004: 195–6). Thus, for opponents, the only meaningful difference between temporary and permanent taxation is that temporary taxation passes more easily through the legislature because of its perceived shorter duration and superficial satisfaction of budgetary rules. The common circumstance, however, is routine extension and actual circumvention of budgetary rules. For these reasons, i.e., ease of passage, budget rule circumvention, and legislative inertia, opponents of temporary taxation argue that its use generally promotes irresponsible fiscal imbalances.

On the other hand, there is a small number of scholars who make the opposite argument. They observe that a permanent spending increase or tax cut hides its full budgetary cost because it only accounts for annual changes against a baseline estimate for the length of the budget window, currently set at ten years. In contrast, a temporary spending increase or tax cut requires reenactment every few years, and therefore typically fits within the budget window for its entire life. Because each reenactment fits within the budget window, a temporary change to the tax code continually subjects itself to budgetary approval under Congressional offsetting rules. Unlike temporary changes, permanent changes require enactment only once, and therefore avoid accounting for those costs which extend beyond the ten year budget window. Temporary changes to the tax code should then be favored in order to promote fiscal balances (Yin 2009).

As already mentioned, most of the scholarship contends that temporary changes do not continually require budgetary approval under Congressional offsetting rules, however. Because American budgetary law is controlled by the legislature itself, budgetary rules are weakly binding and easily circumvented. Critics of temporary taxation have documented how weaknesses have led to shifting baselines, exceptions to offset requirements, and a general flouting of budgetary rules since their introduction (Kysar 2011). These critics assert that any purported benefit which results from ensuring that each temporary enactment continually subjects itself to budgetary rules is therefore meaningless.

The unmet challenge for opponents of temporary taxation has been to suggest a workable constraint that either prohibits the use of temporary tax legislation for avoiding budget restrictions, or that at least forces the legislature to observe the initially legislated duration of a temporary change through the foreclosure of extensions.[2] The difficulty of that challenge is high. The American constitution treats extensions of temporary tax bills like any other legislative enactment. Passage through the legislature and approval by the executive are sufficient for codification. Nor have opponents attempted to craft a coherent legal challenge to those initial enactments of temporary taxation that are deliberately intended to flout budget law. These limitations have led opponents to softly suggest that the legislature should face a rebuttable default rule that requires all tax legislation to be passed permanently (Kysar 2011). Proponents have suggested a rebuttable default rule that requires all tax legislation to be passed temporarily (Yin 2009).

In a detailed critique of Kysar (2011), Professor Epstein emphasizes the inability of default timing rules to constrain lawmakers from seeking rents in exchange for tax legislation (Epstein 2011). He asserts that any second-tier rule related to the organization of the adminstrative state (in this instance, a default rule that favors permanent tax legislation) cannot confine what the legislature can do as a substantive matter (in this instance, to use their discretion to rebut and continue to pass temporary tax legislation). Within the context

---

2 Other solutions that have been suggested include accounting for temporary changes as permanent (Garrett 2004) and setting the length of the budget window to minimize the legislature's incentive to use sunsets in order to avoid budget restrictions (Auerbach 2006). Auerbach (2006) and Yin (2009) discuss the difficulty of using long-term estimates instead of budget window estimates.

of the modern adminstrative state, argues Epstein, the legislature has too many degrees of freedom available to circumvent the substantive purpose of a procedural rule. Permanent default rules will not suffice because they are not strong enough to prevent interest groups from successfully bargaining with the legislature for temporary tax legislation and its extension; temporary default rules will not suffice because they are not strong enough to prevent interest groups from successfully bargaining with the legislature for exemptions.

As already suggested, most of the scholarship on temporary tax legislation takes a strong, and often strident, normative stance against temporary spending increases and tax cuts. The tone reflects a general understanding that temporary changes to the tax code fail to lead to increased fiscal responsibility because of routine extensions. Worse, the relatively shorter duration of those changes makes it politically easier for the legislature to pass spending increases and tax cuts in their first instance, which may contribute to structural increases in long-term deficit levels. On the other hand, proponents point out that each of the initial temporary changes and extensions must adhere to budget rules – weakly binding or not. Yet the literature has only given cursory attention as to why the extensions are routine. Nor has it examined whether the inertia of temporary tax legislation outweighs its questionably weak obligation to incremental cost-accounting. In other words, does the increased ease of passage and extension of temporary tax law relative to permanent tax law outweigh the advantage of confining most temporary changes to tax law within the budget window. Professor Epstein's critique asserts that incremental cost-accounting with an offset requirement (or any other procedural budget constraint) will not adequately check bargaining between the legislature and interest groups, which he implies is socially costly. Thus, the constraining benefits of temporary taxation are illusory.

We consider the problem nonetheless for three reasons. First, we question Epstein's assumption that bargaining between the legislature and interest groups is always socially costly. Second, procedural normative recommendations that flow from an analysis of how exactly contemporary legislatures are using temporary tax legislation can be worthwhile, even if those recommendations take the form of second-tier procedural frameworks like default rules. As Professor Garrett has observed, "[p]rocedural frameworks . . . give [legislators] the opportunity to deliberate and . . . increase the chance that voters will be able to hold their representatives accountable" (Garrett 1998:

567–8). While legislators may not take that opportunity and continue to allow their legislative decisionmaking to be dominated by the acquisition of personal benefits that accrue from bargaining with interest groups, knowledge of ideal solutions can exert pressure on their decisionmaking through other channels such as voter accountability or nonpecuniary legislator utility. Lastly, procedural normative recommendations can have meaningful effects if implemented at the constitutional level. Indeed, there is a growing trend to address fiscal policy constitutionally. Within the past decade, Austria, Germany, Switzerland, and Spain have amended their constitutions with fiscal rules. In the United States, constitutional law scholars have begun to acknowledge that the general intellectual constraints placed upon amendment are largely misplaced, and that amendment should be seriously considered irrespective of the structural difficulties posed by Article V (Vermeule 2009: 165–8). For these reasons, we are interested in developing a thorough understanding of the social costs and benefits of temporary and permanent taxation. We are particularly interested in comparing how each timing rule impacts rent-seeking, private investment, and legislators' reelection strategy.

5.2 COST–BENEFIT ANALYSIS

An analysis of the social costs and benefits of taxation is part of the generalized public finance problem of optimal public spending (Samuelson, P. A. 1954). Solutions to this problem necessarily involve normative questions of how governments should allocate resources intertemporally since borrowing and spending occur over time. It is generally agreed that current generations should, to some extent, limit paying for frontloaded benefits with backloaded costs, but governments have struggled to find the right method to control public spending and budget deficits. Non-constitutional experiments in Europe and the United States have included annual deficit limits, debt–GDP targets, compulsory balanced budgets, target discretionary spending limits, and the current American approach of placing limits on incremental changes to the deficit.[3] Each of the rules embodied in these

[3] See, e.g., Stability and Growth Pact, EU, 1997; Gramm-Rudman-Hollings Balanced Budget and Emergency Deficit Control Act of 1985, 2

experiments has been either bypassed or directly violated, however, and most of the supporting law has been either hollowed out or repealed.

The primary objective of budget rules is to decrease the shifting of future burdens to future generations. As such, the rules attempt to pressure those in control to minimize preemptive borrowing and spending. One reason why legislators borrow and spend preemptively is to foreclose competing legislators from capturing resources. Auerbach (2006) builds a model where two groups, *D* and *R*, differ in preferences over public spending. For example, *D* prefers "big" government with high taxes and high direct spending. *R* prefers "small" government with equally high values of gross taxation, which are reduced by tax expenditures that limit the tax burdens of select classes of constituents. While each group cares fully about its heirs, each nonetheless feels compelled to shortchange them because any resources that could be left to them might first be captured by the competing group. Our analysis of how temporary taxation impacts long-term deficit levels also supposes that two groups, *D* and *R*, differ in preferences over public spending. However, we shift the emphasis away from preemptively capturing tangible resources that take the form of spending increases and tax cuts, and toward capturing political resources which control whether an opponent pays a political cost during an election. Like Auerbach (2006), our analysis supposes that each group cares fully about its heirs, but each feels the need to remain in power through using temporary preemptive borrowing and spending. Temporary tax policy shifts the political costs of applying fiscal discipline onto future political opponents. When the temporary policy expires, legislators pay a political cost if they exercise fiscal discipline and reject an extension. By rejecting extension of a deficit-increasing temporary policy, legislators lose votes from supporters of those policies. At the same time, legislators lose votes from opponents if they choose to extend. Because current-period legislators understand that their political opponents will pay political costs through rejection or extension, current-period legislators choose to preemptively borrow and spend, especially when future control of the legislature is more likely to be at stake.

USC § 900 (2006); Budget Enforcement Act of 1990, Pub. L. No. 101-508, 104 Stat. 1388-573 (codified as amended at scattered sections of 2 USC & 15 USC § 1022).

On the other hand, if legislators choose to preemptively borrow and spend in order to favor one group, they may need to redistribute public resources away from another group through tax increases or reductions in public spending. Thus, any political support gained from favoring one group may be counterbalanced by political opposition gained from disfavoring another group. Under current budget rules of the 112th American Congress, the legislature may not increase spending or cut taxes unless it reduces current public spending. This offset requirement is known as CUTGO, short for cut-as-you-go. Previously, in the 111th Congress, new spending or tax cut legislation could be offset through a reduction in spending or an increase in taxes. This rule was known as PAYGO, short for pay-as-you-go. Under either set of rules, however, offset requirements may be sufficiently weakened so that spending can be increased or taxes can be cut without offsetting reductions in spending or increases in taxes. Before introducing our cost–benefit analysis, we first explain how CUTGO or PAYGO offset requirements are sometimes avoided.

Offset requirements

There are two categories of Congressional offset requirements: actual revenue offsets within the budget window, and a general limit on significant deficit increases that accumulate beyond the budget window. The general limit, known as the Byrd Rule, is applied with discretion by the Senate.[4] While the actual revenue offset rule purports to be mandatory, it too is applied with discretion by the House of Representatives. As mentioned above, the CUTGO rule requires that the cost of new spending or tax cut legislation be offset through a spending reduction. Otherwise, the House may not consider the legislation. The cost of the legislation is measured by calculating the difference in government revenues or outlays with and without the proposed legislation in effect. The latter is known as the baseline. Critically, the cost calculation is only made over the length of the budget window. Any costs that occur beyond the budget window

---

[4] It is applied with discretion because it requires a member of the Senate to raise a point of order if the proposed legislation will substantially increase the deficit beyond the budget window. If no senator raises a point of order, however, the proposed legislation may be considered irrespective of its long-term budgetary impact.

Table 5.1 A shifting baseline for a five-year tax cut

	Years 1–5	Years 6–10	Years 11–20
Baseline (unshifted)	$x - 1$	x	x
Baseline treatment	T	T	T
Required offset to continue tax	–	1	1
Baseline (shifted)	$x - 1$	$x - 1$	$x - 1$
Baseline treatment	T	P	P
Required offset to continue tax	–	0	0

are unaccounted for, and therefore do not require offsets. If the budget window costs are positive, then the House cannot consider the legislation.

However, this rule can be enforced only if a legislator affirmatively raises a point of order. Moreover, with approval from a simple majority, the House Rules Committee can adopt ad hoc rules that waive any points of order when considering budgetary legislation. In short, the budget window offset requirement can be overcome by a majority of controlling legislators. In addition, an affirmative vote by two-thirds of the House can suspend all House Rules, including those that govern points of order.

Kysar (2011) explains a further way that offset requirements can be sufficiently weakened. Usually, the baseline estimate assumes that permanent laws will continue forever and that temporary laws will expire as scheduled. For example, if a temporary tax cut of 1 lowered the baseline to $x - 1$, and was scheduled to expire next year, the baseline for the following year would be x. Recently, however, both the Bush and Obama Presidential Budgets proposed that temporary tax cuts be treated as permanent, despite their adoption as temporary. This means that a permanent extension of the tax cut would be scored with zero costs because it is included in calculating the baseline.

Table 5.1 demonstrates how a shifting baseline can eliminate offset requirements mandated by Congressional rules such as CUTGO. In the upper half of the table, a temporary five-year tax cut with a value of 1 is passed. The baseline accordingly is reduced by 1, and offset rules require the legislature to increase the budget revenues (through a decrease in spending) by 1 in order to pass the tax cut. When the tax cut expires in year 6 or year 11, a further offset of 1 will

Table 5.2 A shifting baseline for an increase in revenues

	Years 1–5	Year 6	Years 7–16
Baseline (unshifted)	$x - 1$	$x - 1$	x
Treatment	T	T	T
Revenues	-1×5	-1×1	0×9
Total gain/loss to the baseline	−5	−1	0
Baseline (shifted)	$x - 1$	x	x
Treatment	T	P	P
Revenues	-1×5	1×1	1×9
Total gain/loss to the baseline	−5	1	9

be required if Congress wishes to extend the tax. This is because the baseline treatment of the tax throughout its life is temporary.

Consider instead the lower half of the table. A temporary five-year tax cut with a value of 1 is passed. The baseline accordingly is reduced by 1, and offset rules require the legislature to increase budget revenues by 1 in order to pass the tax cut. However, in year 6 Congress treats that tax cut as permanent simply because it adopts the President's proposed budget. Because the tax cut is treated as permanent, it no longer requires an increase in budget revenues for its extension. The required offset to continue the tax therefore is 0.

Moreover, once the baseline is shifted, any extension that lasts for less than the length of the budget window would be calculated as an increase in revenues. Thus, if the five-year tax cut were extended for only one more year, the savings across the remaining nine years of the budget window could be used to increase spending or cut taxes somewhere else in the budget.

The upper half of Table 5.2 shows how revenues are calculated for a temporary tax cut, scored at 1 per year, when the baseline remains unshifted. Revenues are reduced by −5 over years 1 through 5, and offset rules require the legislature to increase revenues by 5. At year 6, the tax cut is extended for one year. Because the tax cut is treated as temporary, its extension is scored as reducing revenues by 1 for year 6. At year 7, the tax cut is no longer extended, and the baseline for years 7 through 16 remains unaffected.

Now consider the lower half of the table. Like the unshifted baseline scenario, the tax cut for the first five years is scored at 1 per year. Revenues are accordingly reduced by −5, and offset rules require the legislature to increase revenues by 5 in order to pass the tax cut. At year 6, however, baseline calculations treat the temporary tax cut as permanent. Failing to extend the tax cut in year 6 therefore leads to an increase in revenues of 1. Failing to extend the tax cut over the remainder of a ten-year budget window leads to an increase in revenues of 9.

In sum, offset requirements can be avoided through refusal to raise a point of order, ad hoc rules adopted by the House Rules Committee, a suspension of House rules, and shifting baselines. Thus, our analysis allows legislators to pass new spending or tax cuts by sufficiently weakening offset requirements in addition to reducing current spending (CUTGO and PAYGO) or increasing taxes (PAYGO only).

Benefits and costs

Given baseline spending and taxing levels, a current majority, by passing a new spending increase or tax cut, can create a public benefit (G_1) for the length of the budget window. Suppose this benefit lasts for the length of the budget window with certainty, and will not be extended. The benefit is accompanied by a cost, which can be paid in several ways. First, the benefit can be paid through a redistribution of benefits and costs throughout the length of the budget window. Consider two groups, *D* and *R*. One group receives the benefits of a new spending increase or tax cut; the other group pays the costs of that increase or cut through an increase in their taxes (PAYGO) or a decrease in outstanding government spending that benefits them (PAYGO or CUTGO). Because the public benefit G_1 only lasts for the length of the budget window, the costs (T_1) only last for the length of the budget window also. Because this newly created public benefit is a redistribution between two groups that lasts for a finite period of time with certainty, the joint-welfare impact (W) of this new spending increase or tax cut may be represented by:

$$W = G_{1D} - T_{1R} = 0 \tag{5.1}$$

Now suppose the current majority can circumvent existing budget rules and create a public benefit for the length of the budget window without paying any budget window period costs. As explained above, this can be accomplished through refusal to raise a point of order, ad hoc rules adopted by the House Rules Committee, a suspension of House rules, or shifting the baseline. Assume again that the public benefit lasts for the length of the budget window with certainty. The costs of this public benefit are instead incurred in a time period beyond the budget window. Under this form of temporary tax law, the realization of benefits is immediate, though the realization of costs is delayed:

$$W = G_{1D} - T_{2R} = -S_W \tag{5.2}$$

Unlike the scenario represented by equation 5.1, the cost of the public benefit for group D creates a net joint-welfare loss $-S_W$. This loss represents the cost of servicing debt beyond the budget window that was created by the spending increase or tax cut G_{1D}. Because the current majority chooses to finance G_1 with an offsetting spending cut or tax increase in period 2, the current majority must borrow to create G_1 in period 1. As a result, society as a whole must pay financing costs for G_1 in addition to group R's period-2 outlay.[5]

5.2.1 The Normative Neutrality of Rent Extraction

Now suppose that the public benefit is not confined to the budget window with certainty. It can either expire as it does in equations 5.1 and 5.2, or it can be extended. Kysar (2011) notes that the possibility of extension leads to higher levels of interaction between legislators and interest groups when compared with permanent tax legislation. Because the temporary public benefit will expire, interest groups will lobby legislators to continue that benefit each time the law is about to sunset. Instead, if the public benefit were legislated permanently, interaction between legislators and interest groups would occur only once, at the law's enactment. Each time the legislators and interest groups interact following a temporary enactment, legislators are able to extract payments from an interest group in exchange for continuing a beneficial spending increase or tax cut (McChesney 1997; Eskridge et al. 2006: 97). Using our shorthand, the difference according to Kysar (2011) is

[5] Even when relaxing the assumption that D and R differ in preferences over public spending, circumvention of budget rules creates a net social cost of debt service.

$$W_\tau = m\,(G_D - T_R) = m\,(-R_D) \qquad (5.3)$$

$$W\pi = G_D - T_R = 0 \qquad (5.4)$$

For m interactions that follow the initial enactment, a total rent of $m\,(-R_D)$ is extracted. Note that the rent is extracted from the group which receives the public benefit only. This theory creates a compelling normative argument against temporary tax legislation and in favor of permanent tax legislation since the joint-welfare impact of permanent legislation (W_π) is 0. From our explication, however, it is clear that rent extraction simply reduces the size of the public benefit at the expense of the beneficiary, and not at the expense of society as a whole. Thus, the social impact of the temporary tax is better understood as $W_T = m\,(G_D - T_R - R_D) = 0$.

It is straightforward that the beneficiary, and not society as a whole, pays the extracted rent. Interest groups make payments in exchange for legislation that benefits them. Any additional benefits that accrue to other groups are external to the transaction. Legislators cannot extract rents from other groups by supplying them with legislation because those other groups are not actively demanding legislation. For example, if D demands legislation, legislators cannot ask for payments in exchange from R. R would not agree to make payments precisely because R does not demand the legislation.

Worse, a normative theory of rent extraction used against temporary taxation cannot show that the increased potential for rent extraction under temporary legislation may reduce the level of beneficial externalities created by a legislative transaction. Beneficial externalities are benefits that accrue to a group that is not involved in the legislative transaction. For example, an interest group may successfully bargain for an extension of the R&D tax credit. If the individual firms that make up that interest group hire additional researchers as a result of their reduced taxes, the additional researchers, who by assumption must benefit from that employment more than they benefit from their current employment, are said to receive benefits that are external to the legislative transaction. Importantly, the newly employed researchers did not expend any resources to bargain for the R&D tax credit, but they nonetheless benefit from its passage. Opponents of temporary taxation might argue that because D would make additional payments for legislation, D may demand less legislation that could have socially beneficial effects for *R* like those that accrue to our hypothetical researchers.[6] As a result, rent extraction under a series of temporary extensions would not only reduce the welfare of *D*, but also that of *R*.

A reduction in joint-welfare is ambiguous, however. First, it is unlikely that *D* will demand significantly lower levels of legislation. This is because legislators are extracting a portion of the legislation consumer surplus in a negotiation context. The consumer surplus involved in a transaction for legislation is the benefit that exceeds the interest group's willingness to pay. For example, if the interest group is willing to pay $100 million for an extension of the R&D tax credit because it will receive that amount in rent, and expends $1 million in payments to legislators in order to negotiate the extension, then the interest group's consumer surplus is the difference between its willingness to pay and the payment, i.e. $99 million. If legislators are able to extract additional rent, that is, through negotiating payments for extension, then the consumer surplus will shrink as a result. When legislators negotiate additional payments for extensions, the price of legislation is not simply increasing and exerting a downward pressure on demand; legislators are interacting with interest groups and learning what those interest groups are willing to pay for an extension of temporary legislation before setting the price. While legislators may engage in price discrimination, they cannot prohibitively price the legislation in order to receive their payments. Thus, the supply of spending increase and tax cut extensions is unlikely to significantly decrease due to rent extraction. This means that any socially beneficial effects that accrue to *R* from extensions demanded by *D* are unlikely to decrease in any meaningful way.

A theory of rent extraction therefore cannot positively show that temporary taxation unambiguously reduces social welfare; it can only show that a particular group that demands legislation could potentially pay a price closer to its actual willingness to pay. Moreover, under the assumption of consensual transacting, interest

---

6 We would need to relax the assumption that *D* and *R* have divergent interests. The theory is further complicated by the fact that because the beneficiary *R* is not actively seeking the legislation desired by *D*, a subjective value of the legislation must be imputed to *R* in order to determine *R*'s valuation of the legislation, and *R*'s consequent valuation of the beneficial externality brought on by *D*'s effort.

groups always receive a net gain at each extension. Otherwise, they would not transact.[7] This means that any additional payment made by interest groups under a series of temporary extensions simply reduces the legislative consumer surplus that might be experienced under a permanent enactment. Under temporary legislation, legislators may capture a greater portion of that surplus; under permanent legislation, the lion's share may go to the interest group.

Aside from the fact that anchoring a theory against temporary taxation in rent-seeking requires normative argument that favors a particular interest group over a controlling group of legislators, it is not entirely clear that the total outlay made by an interest group for multiple extensions would exceed the total outlay for a permanent enactment. Under a permanent timing rule, group *D* receives an infinite stream of benefits. Under a temporary timing rule, group *D* receives a finite stream of benefits. If interest groups are paying for legislation in benefits, then they presumably would pay more for a permanent enactment because it offers a larger stream of benefits (Gersen 2007). Thus, the total outlay for a temporary enactment and multiple extensions may not exceed the total outlay for a permanent enactment. When this is true, rent extraction through a series of temporary extensions is less appealing to legislators. They can receive a larger payment in exchange for permanent passage up front. In either case, a legislative transaction necessarily involves a wealth transfer between legislators and interest groups. Absent a strong normative argument that recognizes that interest groups should receive a larger portion of the legislative consumer surplus, temporary and permanent taxation present an ambiguous comparison of social benefits and costs in terms of rent extraction.

There is an additional benefit of temporary taxation worth mentioning in the rent extraction context. At each extension, the interest group may exchange information with lawmakers about why continuance of the public benefit is merited. As explained in chapter 4, lawmakers use information in order to create better-informed laws,

---

7 See Posner, R. A. (1983: 88). Posner demonstrates the concept of consensual transacting with the example of a greengrocer: "If A sells a tomato to B for $2 . . ., we can be sure that the utility to A of $2 is greater than the utility of the tomato to him, and vice versa for B." Likewise, if an interest group trades payments for a legislative extension, we can be sure that its utility of the extension is greater than its utility of the payments.

which can have positive impacts on social welfare. Early signaling models of lobby activity recognize the social value of information transmitted through lobbying. Later research goes further, showing that regulatory capture can enhance welfare since capture may entail closer relationships between interest groups and legislators, thereby promoting higher levels of informal interaction that produces hard-to-get and socially valuable information (Coglianese et al. 2004). Even if we were to accept the normative argument that interest groups should claim a greater portion of the legislative consumer surplus via permanent legislation, that benefit would still need to be balanced against the loss of information that is revealed by the interest group at each interaction under the temporary-legislation cost structure.

In sum, the comparison between temporary and permanent taxation with respect to rent extraction cannot unambiguously identify a loss in joint-welfare. Instead, the comparison involves a normative argument over who should receive greater claim to the legislative consumer surplus. Under temporary tax legislation, legislators may capture a greater portion if they successfully extract a series of rents. Under permanent tax legislation, the interest group may capture a greater portion. Still, the total outlay under a series of smaller temporary enactments may be less than the total outlay under a larger permanent enactment. Nonetheless, opponents of temporary taxation have argued that permanent taxation should be favored because it creates less opportunity for rent extraction. They view rent extraction as costly to society. By contrast, if we view rent extraction as merely a wealth transfer between legislators and interest groups, then temporary tax legislation is unambiguously welfare-improving because higher levels of interaction can lead to information production. Temporary tax legislation increases the level of interaction between lawmakers and interest groups, which increases the possibility that beneficial information for lawmaking will be revealed.

5.2.2 The Ambiguous Cost of Uncertainty

The legislature's discretion to extend or not extend temporary tax legislation creates an uncertain environment, which can undermine the effectiveness of intended tax incentives, particularly those aimed at the promotion of long-term investment or the adjustment of behavior that requires significant commitment (Yin 2009). While permanent legislation can be repealed or amended, temporary legislation automatically expires without affirmative action by the legislature, and may create less-certain legal environments than those created by permanent legislation as a result. That temporary legislation can create less-certain legal environments than permanent legislation is not always true, however.

As we saw in chapter 4, temporary enactments can signal a long-term legislative commitment when the legislature is continually adjusting legislation to a changing legal environment. Because adjustments to temporary legislation incur less transactions cost than adjustments to permanent legislation, interest groups that expect legislators to adjust statutes know that temporary enactments signal a legislative commitment toward achieving a particular policy objective (lemma 5). Consider a policy to curb the number of highway deaths through an optimal speed limit, for example. Suppose the legislature has a history of adjusting the limit laws according to highway fatality statistics and that interest groups expect the legislature to continue to adjust the law so as to minimize deaths. When the legislature passes a temporary bill setting the limit to 75 miles per hour for one year, it signals that it is likely to adjust the limit again based upon the number of highway deaths at the 75 miles per hour limit. Had the legislature enacted the limit permanently, it would need to expend transactions cost for placement of the adjustment on the legislative agenda in addition to expending the transactions cost for amendment. Through an enactment of a permanent measure, interest groups would know that the commitment to setting an optimal limit has been weakened. This is true because a cost-minimizing legislature would prefer to avoid the cost of agenda placement and amendment if it intended to adjust the law at a later date. Given that adjustment to a permanent enactment is marginally more costly than adjustment to a temporary enactment, cost-minimizing legislatures signal that they are serious about adjusting the law and getting it right only if they enact the law temporarily.[8]

[8] Of course if the transactions cost of agenda placement and amendment under a permanent timing rule equal the transactions cost of a new enactment under a temporary timing rule, the signal would have no content. The point here is that there can exist circumstances where a temporary timing rule can increase certainty with respect to a policy objective under a realistic set of assumptions.

Thus, a temporary enactment signals a long-term legislative commitment to an underlying policy (e.g., limiting highway fatalities) and can therefore provide certainty with respect to that policy.

Yin (2009) provides two additional scenarios where temporary tax policies provide certainty. First, when the legislature guarantees a tax benefit for investments made on a particular day, i.e. through a "grandfather clause," the certainty of that temporary tax benefit is perfect. Interest groups are guaranteed a tax benefit when they take action on a particular day regardless of whether the tax benefit expires or extends at a later date. Second, repeated extensions of a tax benefit over a sufficient amount of time can create certainty that the same benefit will be extended again. For example, the research and development tax credit has been extended over twenty times since the 1980s, and interest groups may expect the credit to be extended again as a result. Thus, overall it is unclear that permanent tax policies provide higher levels of certainty than temporary tax policies. Temporary tax policies do not dampen socially desirable actions that require long-term commitments, like investment, in every instance. Other parameters must be considered.

Moreover, higher levels of uncertainty can lead to higher levels of investment. In general, and outside of the tax context, the literature recognizes that uncertainty can increase or decrease investment levels. If an investment is reversible, that is, if the outlay can be redirected toward a different investment at a later date with no cost, then uncertain and favorable conditions increase investment levels (Abel 1983). The capital can simply be costlessly redirected toward another use, and there is no potential for loss in the initial investment. In this scenario, investors still realize gains during temporary and favorable conditions even if the investment environment turns out to be unfavorable in the long term. For example, temporary and favorable conditions in fuel oil consumption may increase investment in petroleum exploration and production to serve the fuel oil market. If fuel oil consumption decreases, the product of exploration and production investment, i.e. petroleum, can simply be redirected to other types of petroleum consumers such as petrochemical producers. The initial investment spurred by favorable conditions in fuel oil consumption experiences no loss as it is costlessly redirected. From a broad perspective, favorable conditions for petroleum consumption in general have never declined, but the point is that the uncertain investment in fuel oil production can be reversed, and any loss in an initial investment in fuel oil can therefore be avoided. Generally this means that even if the environment is uncertain, investment will increase as long as it is reversible.

When investment is irreversible, the investor will balance the expected costs of waiting for a certain environment to arrive against the expected costs of investing in an uncertain environment today (Dixit and Pindyck 1994). For example, an investment in specialized higher education is irreversible because it cannot be redirected toward a different specialty at a later date. Suppose conditions are uncertain because the value of specialized education can increase or decrease depending upon job market conditions. When job market conditions are favorable but uncertain, investment levels will not necessarily increase because the education cannot be redirected if conditions deteriorate. A potential student will consider the expected costs of waiting for favorable and certain job market conditions, measured for example in foregone income while waiting for favorable and certain conditions. If those costs are greater than the expected costs of investing in education in a favorable and uncertain environment, measured perhaps in the cost of holding a potentially worthless education upon matriculation, then the student will make the education investment. A student who estimates the costs of waiting for certainty to be greater than the costs of failing under uncertainty will choose to invest. In general, investors balance the expected costs of waiting for a certain environment to arrive against the expected costs of investing in an uncertain environment today. Thus, investment levels may still increase in uncertain environments even when investment is irreversible, but not always.

Hassett and Metcalf (1999) consider investment in an uncertain policy environment for investment tax credits. They find that increases in uncertainty can increase irreversible investment. This is because investment tax credits typically offer benefits beyond the status quo rate of return on an investment. If a credit is not extended, the tax environment does not worsen with respect to the original investment environment. It simply reverts to the status quo. Given that a status quo rate of return is sufficient to spur investment, uncertainty surrounding increases to that rate through tax credits will not decrease investment. On the contrary, uncertainty will spur investment further because an investor will want to use the tax credits today fearing that they will not be available tomorrow. The same rationale applies to temporary reduction in tax rates. If a reduction fails to be extended, the tax rate does not become unfavorable with respect to the original investment environment, it simply reverts to the status quo tax rate. Given that the status quo tax rate still spurs investment, uncertainty surrounding an extension of the rate reduction will not decrease investment. Investors, fearing that they may lose the favorable rate reduction, will increase investment in order to take advantage of it. Generally, as Professor Yin notes, favorable and uncertain tax policies that revert to the status quo create a "use-it or lose-it effect" and increase irreversible investment (Yin 2009: 246).

In contrast, unfavorable and uncertain tax policies that revert to the status quo may decrease irreversible investment if the value of waiting for reversion exceeds any gain that can be made on the investment under the unfavorable measures. Temporary elimination of deductions or credits, or temporary increases in tax rates, for example, may decrease irreversible investment if the value of waiting for the more favorable status quo tax environment exceeds any forgone returns under those less favorable conditions. Overall, like the general result for irreversible investment in favorable and uncertain conditions described in Hassett and Metcalf (1999), investment levels may still increase in unfavorable and uncertain tax environments even when investment is irreversible, but not always.

In sum, temporary tax policies may or may not introduce uncertainty. Temporary tax policies can signal long-term commitments in policy adjustment contexts, they can provide guaranteed benefits through grandfather clauses, and they can be routinely extended and lead to sufficiently high expectations of certainty. When temporary tax policies do introduce uncertainty, investment may or may not decrease. If investment is reversible without cost, investment will not decrease. If investment is irreversible, investment will not decrease if the uncertain conditions are favorable and revert to the status quo. If investment is irreversible, but uncertain conditions are unfavorable and revert to the status quo, investment will decrease only if the value of waiting for reversion to the status quo exceeds the value of forgone investment under the less favorable conditions. All of this points to a general ambiguity in the social cost of uncertainty introduced by temporary tax measures.

5.2.3 The Unambiguous Cost of Reelection Strategy

In the introductory part of section 5.2, we noted that Auerbach (2006) develops a model where one group *D* prefers to shortchange its heirs through preemptive borrowing and spending because any economic resources that may be left to them could first be captured by a competing group *R*. While the capture of future group resources may be one plausible explanation for preemptive borrowing and spending, a more immediate and pressing concern for a legislator is reelection. Legislators can increase their chances of reelection by using temporary tax legislation strategically.

When legislators pass temporary tax cuts or spending increases, they guarantee that future legislators must decide to extend or not extend them. At expiration, future legislators pay a political cost if they exercise fiscal discipline and reject extensions. By rejecting an extension of temporary tax cuts or spending increases, legislators lose votes from supporters of those cuts and increases. At the same time, future legislators pay political costs for extending. For example, representatives of group *D* pay political costs for extending the tax cuts of group *R*, or representatives of group *R* pay political costs for extending the spending increases of group *D*. Because current-period legislators understand that their rivals will pay political costs through rejection or extension, current period legislators preemptively borrow and spend thereby forcing their rivals to incur political costs.

While the political choice to extend or not extend can create benefits in addition to costs, the creation of those benefits is in the hands of the current legislature which passes (or extends) the temporary tax legislation. Current-period legislators will not create expected political opportunities for their rivals, and as a result, most temporary tax legislation used for political jockeying is likely to create net political costs, and not net political benefits, for second-period rivals. Figure 5.1 outlines the strategy for a current period legislator.

Nature moves first and chooses whether the legislator represents group *D* with probability γ or *R* with probability $1 - \gamma$. The legislator then chooses to preemptively borrow and spend temporarily (tt), i.e. create or extend temporary tax legislation, or not ($-tt$). With probability p the election is contested. With probability $1 - p$, the election is a landslide. The payoffs are straightforward. Current-period legislators always win in a landslide, but if their reelection is

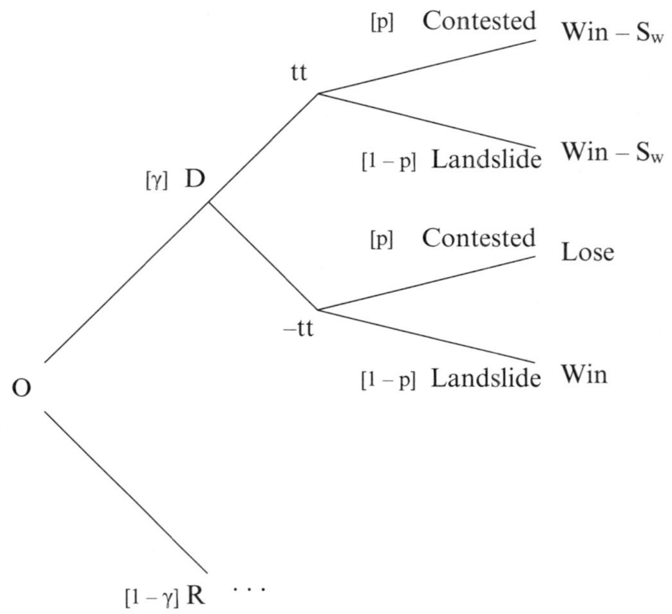

Figure 5.1 Reelection through temporary taxation

contested, their taxing strategy impacts the outcome. If we assume that a contested election hangs upon the votes of the group which is adversely impacted by a rejection to extend tax legislation, then by backward induction, the optimal strategy for current-period legislators is to create or extend tax legislation (*tt*). The payoff for this strategy is reelection. By passing temporary tax legislation today, current-period legislators create political costs for their rivals and perhaps for themselves, but rivals' costs are likely to be greater. Rivals must extend temporary tax legislation that favors the opposing group because the outcome of the election hangs upon the votes that support extension. Yet if they do so, they lose the support of their own group. Instead, current-period legislators also must extend temporary tax legislation that favors their own group. Yet if they do so, they do not lose the support of their own group. For this reason, the political costs of rejecting or extending are likely to be greater for rivals than the political costs of extending for current-period legislators. In a contested election, the difference yields the payoff $(W_{in} - S_w)$ for current-period legislators who choose the strategy (*tt*). In addition, if the temporary tax legislation creates a benefit (G_{1D}) with a delayed cost (T_{2R}) through the avoidance of offset requirements, then a social cost $-S_W$ for debt service is incurred as it is in equation 5.2. As the probability p of a contested election decreases, the legislator is more likely to choose to not preemptively borrow and spend temporarily, given a legislative preference for reducing social cost. In other words, if legislators are socially benevolent and prefer to limit paying for frontloaded benefits with backloaded debt servicing costs, then they will choose to not preemptively borrow and spend temporarily as likelihood of winning in a landslide increases.

By examining temporary tax legislation in relation to reelection incentives, it is easy to see why avoiding spending offset requirements can be so critical to a legislator's strategy. For in a contested election that marginally hangs upon the extension of tax legislation, it is likely that the gain of political support from one group which benefits from extension will counterbalance the loss of political support from another group which must pay for that extension with an offsetting spending decrease (or tax increase). Indeed, the rationale for offset requirements is to render legislative adjustments to prevailing tax policy budget neutral. If adjustments affect groups which are able to change reelection outcomes, then offset requirements that favor one group over another are not only budget neutral, but politically neutral as well. By avoiding offset requirements, however, political benefits accrue to current-period legislators (and financial benefits accrue to favored groups) at the expense of political costs that accrue to second-period rivals (and debt servicing costs that accrue to the public). In this way, temporary tax legislation that avoids offset requirements can alter the outcome of a contested reelection.

Even if budgetary offset requirements are avoided, extension could still be politically costly thereby eliminating any political gains to the legislator. For example, legislators might pay political costs for extension because they are increasing the debt servicing costs of the public, or because they are continuing the favorable tax policies of partisan rivals. When extending in those scenarios, legislators gain support from proponents of extension, but lose support from opponents. Costs associated with rejecting the extension are likely to be greater than costs associated with supporting the extension, however. This is because temporary tax legislation typically yields concentrated benefits and distributed costs. Benefits concentrate on groups which conduct research and experimentation, produce biodiesel and renewable fuels, maintain railroad tracks, train mine rescue teams, build motorsports entertainment complexes, facilitate child adoptions, educate children at public schools, etc.[9] Instead, the cost of servicing debt, or alternatively, the cost of general partisan dissatisfaction, is widely distributed across the public at large. Revoking concentrated benefits at the expense of creating distributed benefits is generally more politically costly for legislators (Eskridge et al. 2006: 814). Thus, the political cost of failing to extend beneficial temporary taxation is unlikely to be significantly offset by any political benefits due to deficit reduction or widely distributed party satisfaction. As a result, temporary tax legislation that avoids offset requirements is still likely to alter the outcome of a contested reelection.

In sum, current-period legislators who pass temporary tax cuts or spending increases guarantee that future legislators must decide to extend or not extend them. If future-period legislators do not extend, then they lose support from proponents of extension. If they extend, then they lose support from opponents of extension. By backward induction, current-period legislators will pursue temporary tax legislation in order to force their political rivals into difficult positions. As the probability that the election will be contested increases, temporary tax legislation becomes more attractive to current-period legislators because their rivals will be forced to extend cuts and increases that are unpopular with their constituencies. At the margins, the rivals' decision to either extend or not extend will cost them an election.

When current-period legislators pursue this strategy, but are required to offset any tax cuts or spending increases, they too incur political costs. In this way, offset requirements can render temporary tax legislation politically neutral. However, as discussed above, offset requirements can be circumvented thereby creating net political gains. The social cost of using temporary tax legislation without offsets for reelection is unambiguous. The favored group garners a current-period economic benefit, but debt servicing costs accrue at a

[9] For a full list, see Joint Comm. on Taxation, JCX-6-12, Legislative Background of Expiring Federal Tax Provisions 2011–2022 (2012).

later period beyond the budget window. This economic cost is borne by all groups, regardless of their preferences over public spending.

5.3 CONCLUSION

While rent extraction and uncertainty provide unclear normative arguments on the social value of temporary tax legislation, the impact of temporary tax legislation on reelection strategy provides a clear normative argument against its use. To the extent that the scholarship has focused on rent extraction and uncertainty to point to social welfare loss, its normative persuasiveness is arguably misplaced. On the other hand, the use of temporary taxation as a reelection strategy clearly demonstrates social welfare loss. Auerbach (2006) reasons that legislators preemptively borrow and spend to capture future economic resources. This may be true, but a more immediate concern for legislators is reelection. Our analysis clarifies how legislators can use preemptive borrowing and spending in order to create political costs for their rivals, which in turn increases the likelihood of their reelection. This practice is socially costly because it creates costs that are external to the political process, namely, the social cost of servicing debt.

Optimizing the length of the budget window so as to minimize preemptive borrowing and spending, as recommended in Auerbach (2006), will not eliminate the use of temporary tax legislation as a reelection strategy. As explained above, Congressional offset requirements are easily circumvented. Circumvention effectively places costs beyond the budget window irrespective of its length. Thus, any positive impact that an optimal length may have is easily undermined through circumvention devices like ad hoc rules adopted by the House Rules Committee, a suspension of House rules, and shifting baselines.

As Professor Epstein emphasizes, second-tier procedural rules like default presumptions in favor of permanent tax legislation (Kysar 2011), or Congressionally optimized budget windows (Auerbach 2006), cannot meaningfully constrain lawmakers from using temporary tax legislation to seek reelection. Rent-seeking groups simply place too much pressure upon legislators, and it is unrealistic to expect legislators to tie their own hands with a procedural rule that cuts against their reelection (Epstein 2011). Professor Garrett has suggested that procedural frameworks give legislators the opportunity to deliberate and increase the chance that voters will be able to hold them accountable. However, as we have noted above, most temporary tax legislation involves concentrated benefits that immediately impact the economically favored group, and distributed costs that gradually impact the public who provide the debt service. While procedural frameworks may raise the profile of what Professor Garrett refers to as "budget gimmicks," it is unlikely that the diffused public will be able to meaningfully pressure legislators through voting.

Thus it is unlikely that the practice of using temporary tax legislation for reelection can be constrained by legislators. Yet none of the scholarship has discussed judicial or constitutional solutions. This is unsurprising. Certainly, using the tax power for reelection does not satisfy the American constitutional requirement that taxation provide for the general welfare, but attempting to uncloak a tax policy as bare reelection strategy could prove impossible for a court. A constitutional solution, while politically difficult, is at least straightforward. An amendment stipulating that all temporary tax legislation adhere to offset requirements would significantly dampen the ability of legislators to use temporary tax legislation for reelection. However, that solution is problematic because the budget window is currently set at ten years. Offsets that occur beyond the legislators' elected term can still create political costs that occur several years after a temporary tax cut or spending increase is passed. Thus, the rule would need to stipulate that the tax cuts or spending increases and their offsets take immediate effect.[10] Under such an amendment, all temporary borrowing and spending offsets immediately, and each temporary tax adjustment is budget neutral as a result. Additionally, constitutional adherence to immediate offset requirements ensures that any political benefit from favoring one group with a temporary tax cut or spending increase is offset by the political cost of disfavoring another group with a temporary tax increase or spending cut. Thus, an amendment that provides for temporary taxation with immediate offset requirements forces legislators to internalize the political costs that they create, and exerts a downward pressure on using temporary tax legislation for reelection.

---

10 See Luppi and Parisi (2009) for a comparison of immediate versus delay timing rules.

PART II

Evidence

6. Passage probability

6.1 INTRODUCTION

While Part I provides a theory of the selection of temporary and permanent timing rules in various strategic contexts, Part II provides empirical evidence. Chapters 6 and 7 test for the existence of short- to medium-term normative effects and long-term normative effects respectively, and whether or not they vary with the selection of a timing rule. This chapter takes up the first question related to short- to medium-term effects. Proposition 3 shows that the selection of temporary legislation minimizes transactions cost when residual effects such as legal expression cause compliance to increase over time. When compliance is increasing, a temporary timing rule allows legislators to save on total legislation costs since increases in compliance lead to decreases in extension costs of temporary legislation. These cost savings are unavailable with permanent timing rules since permanent enactment costs are allocated to the initial period. In order to test this theory, we measure the level of transactions cost of legislation, and look for variance in those costs over multiple policy domains. Short of developing a full theory of what makes a policy domain more expressive than another, we assume that some policy domains, e.g. judiciary, leave more beneficial residual effects that drive legislation costs down than others, e.g. agriculture.

Transactions cost is measured by performing a binomial logistic regression to estimate the predictors of the likelihood that a bill becomes law, in which we consider characteristics of the bill (including whether it is temporary or permanent) and characteristics of the bill's sponsor as explanatory variables, as well as a set of committee dummies to measure the effect of policy domain. The likelihood that a bill becomes law is used as a proxy for its relative level of transactions cost. Thus, that a bill is more likely to become law than another is indicative of a comparatively lower level of transactions cost. The set of committee dummies provides variance in policy domains and serves as a proxy for varying degrees of beneficial residual effects, i.e. expressivity. If we find that the fixed effect on temporary passage of having originated in one committee is significant and the fixed effect on temporary passage of having originated in another committee is not, we may conclude that there exists an optimal selection of timing rule with respect to transactions cost that varies with committee and by assumption with legal expression.

6.2 THEORY

As stated above, we are interested in how the inclusion of a temporary provision impacts the passage of a bill across committees. Specifically, we model the legislature's binary decision to include or not to include a temporary provision as a function of the probability that a bill becomes law. Our central claim is that the inclusion of a temporary provision increases that probability, irrespective of various characteristics of a bill and its sponsors. Consider a simplified version of the legislative cost function given in chapter 2:

$$l(x, r) = e + m(x, r)$$

where e are enactment costs and m are maintenance costs. Let maintenance costs be given by:

$$m(x, r) = x(a + b^2) + r(y + z^2)$$

where x and r are quadratic extension and repeal cost functions with fixed and marginal components. The fixed components a and y represent the fixed non-bargaining costs that are required for every extension and repeal. The marginal components represent the variable costs that are dependent upon supply-side considerations such as prevailing levels of compliance, opposition, controversy, social norms, and other factors pertaining to the legislation environment.[1]

Suppose a perfectly informed legislature passes a bill with no probability of repeal or extension. A permanent bill would provide

---

[1] These factors can be understood as the aggregate compliance level given by equation 2.14 in chapter 2.

an infinite stream of benefits and a temporary bill would provide a discrete stream of benefits. Holding the substance of the legislation and other factors constant, the value of permanent passage is greater than temporary passage. The difference in their value would only be reflected in the length of the temporary bill and the discount factor of the beneficiary. If legislators are paying for legislation in benefits, a less valued temporary bill will have a lower enactment cost and pass more easily. Suppose instead that a perfectly informed legislature passes a bill of a fixed length and a probability of rescission equal to 1. Under a permanent timing rule, that legislation would incur cost $e + r(y + z^2)$ where r accounts for repeal costs. Under a temporary timing rule, that legislation would incur cost e. Because a temporary bill automatically expires and avoids repeal costs, it provides a lower total cost and should pass more easily. This is true as long as z is weakly positive, i.e. the legislative environment is constant or becomes better.[2]

When there is no probability of repeal and the probability of extension is 1, permanent legislation incurs cost e and temporary legislation incurs cost $e + x(a + b^2)$. Because permanent legislation provides an infinite stream of benefits, e_π is greater than e_τ, but sufficient extension costs x lead to greater total cost temporary legislation. Instead, if x is sufficiently low, a temporary bill should pass more easily. Low x occurs for two reasons. There are few extensions of temporary legislation which keep fixed costs a down, or because the legislative environment is improving which provides constantly decreasing variable costs $-xb^2$. As mentioned above, variable costs are dependent upon supply-side considerations such as prevailing levels of compliance, opposition, controversy, and other factors. When favorable factors are increasing and unfavorable factors are decreasing, legislation becomes easier to extend. These factors are not necessarily exogenous. If the initial enactment is expressive,

---

[2] If the legislative environment worsens, the repeal is a benefit $-rz^2$ that could presumably equate the total costs of a permanent and temporary timing rule where $e_\pi + r(y - z^2) = e_\tau$. Nonetheless, legislators incur fixed repeal costs ry and could also equate total costs by setting e_τ to the appropriate length to balance $-rz^2$. Given a positive discount factor, $e_\pi + r(y - z^2) > e_\tau$ since the repeal $-rz^2$ occurs after the enactment e. Thus a temporary bill should pass more easily as long as the probability of repeal is 1 and the appropriate length of the bill is perfectly known.

the law may affect behavior that is mediated by social norms and lead to increased compliance and decreased opposition (Funk 2007, Feldman 2009). Sufficient decreasing variable extension costs $-xb^2$ permit lower cost temporary legislation even when there is no probability of repeal and the probability of extension is 1. A temporary bill should pass more easily then, if b is negative and of a sufficient magnitude. A permanent bill should pass more easily if extension costs are too great.

This suggests that total legislation costs vary with statutory timing rules, even when legislative substance is held constant, and that there exists an optimum timing rule for a given legislative environment (Landes and Posner 1975, Gersen and Posner 2007, Luppi and Parisi 2009). In order to test this theory, we would ideally want to compare two substantively equivalent bills, one of which contains a temporal restriction, and the other of which does not. If the bills are not substantively alike, it may be that legislators include a temporal restriction in order to increase the passage probability of bills that contain more costly provisions. If so, passage probability may account for the inclusion of the temporal restriction rather than the temporal restriction accounting for the passage probability. Because no two bills are substantively alike, we compare the average passage probability of temporary bills to the average passage probability of permanent bills. We address the possibility that the optimum choice of timing rule varies with policy domain by examining the effect of temporary timing rules on passage probability for bills that originate within various Congressional committees. If the inclusion of a temporary provision more greatly affects the passage probability of bills that originate within some committees compared to others, then the variation demonstrates that temporary timing rules can be optimally selected according to policy domain. Given an expressive effect of law, we might expect a higher probability of temporary passage in say the Judiciary committee as opposed to Veterans Affairs, but again, the results should be interpreted with the caveat that policy domain may be impacting the choice of the temporal restriction.

We are also interested in how total legislation costs vary with statutory timing rules irrespective of the legislative environment. In other words, what features of legislation or its sponsors favor temporary passage instead of permanent passage. To that end, the empirical analysis examines legislation characteristics such as its duration in Congress, and its number of co-sponsors as well as sponsor characteristics such as age, political party, and tenure. We examine whether or not those characteristics significantly affect passage, and whether or not they dampen the impact that the inclusion of a temporary provision has on passage probability.

6.3 DATA AND SUMMARY STATISTICS

We collected data on 1025 bills introduced in the House of Representatives during the 110th Congress. The bills were drawn by simple random sampling from a population of 7366, and represent about 14 percent of the total number of bills introduced between January 3, 2007 and January 3, 2009, the first and last days that Congress was in session. We collected information on passage (i.e. whether the bill became law), the type of bill (i.e. permanent, temporary, or hybrid), the bill's duration in Congress, the bill's sponsor, the bill's number of co-sponsors, and binary information on the committees to which the bill referred. All of this data was collected from the THOMAS database maintained by the Library of Congress. In addition, we collected data on the bill's sponsor from the Biographical Directory of the United States Congress.

Bill characteristics

Out of the randomly sampled 1025 bills, only 76 (7.4 percent) became law; 68.6 percent of the bills were permanent, 17.5 percent were strictly temporary, and 14.0 percent were hybrid bills which contain both permanent and temporary provisions.

Of the 76 bills that became law, 34 (44.7 percent) were permanent, 12 (15.7 percent) were temporary, and 30 (39.4 percent) were hybrid bills. Table 6.1 reports the number of bills that became law

Table 6.1 Number of bills that became law tabulated by type, 110th Congress

Type	Passed (%)	Failed (%)	Total
Permanent	34 (4.84)	669 (95.16)	703
Temporary	12 (6.70)	167 (93.30)	179
Hybrid	30 (20.98)	113 (79.02)	143
Total	76 (7.41)	949 (92.59)	1025

tabulated by type, which reveals that a smaller portion of permanent legislation became law compared to temporary and hybrid types.

The duration of a bill, expressed in days, is computed as the time elapsed between the date of introduction and the date of the last major action. The latter can be the date when a bill becomes law, or the date when a failed bill is last reported or placed on the legislative calendar. When a bill does not pass through a committee, the date of last major action is typically the date the bill is referred to a subcommittee, or the date that the bill is introduced in the House. Bills with higher duration have more time to be deliberated, and at least weakly greater potential to reach consensus than bills which have less time to be deliberated. As a result, we posit a relationship between duration and passage probability.

Because the duration variable is computed as the time elapsed between introduction and last major action, it does not distinguish between relatively early and late introduction of bills. Thus its use as a predictor of the likelihood of bill passage might yield misleading results if this distinction is unaccounted for. For example, a bill that is brought before Congress on its first day in session will have a maximum of 731 days (the duration of the 110th Congress) for reaching a decision whether that bill becomes law. On the other hand, a bill that is introduced on the 300th day of Congress will have a maximum of 431 days for a decision even if both bills had the same actual duration.

To account for this distinction, we have normalized the duration of a bill by taking the ratio of the time elapsed between its introduction and its last major action to the difference between the last day of Congress and the date of the introduction of the bill. This ratio, named real duration, is a continuous variable between 0 and 1, and is simply the duration of the bill divided by the maximum possible duration of the bill, indicating how much of the maximum possible time available is consumed by deliberation. In the sample, on average, only 13 percent of the maximum possible duration available is spent for deliberation of further Congressional action. Upon inspection of the distribution of real duration, 60 percent of the bills have consumed only 5 percent or less of the maximum possible duration, whereas 80 percent of the bills have consumed 25 percent or less of the maximum possible duration.

Sponsor characteristics

In addition to the bill characteristics of passage, type, and duration, we collected data on the sponsor characteristics. Each bill is sponsored by at least one representative and can be co-sponsored by any additional number of the remaining 434 members of the House. For each observation, we collected information on the party of the sponsor, the age and tenure of the sponsor, and the number of co-sponsors. Table 6.2 reports the number of bills that became law tabulated by the party of the sponsor.

The descriptive statistics of the sponsor characteristics are displayed in Table 6.3. The age of a bill's sponsor ranges between 34 and 85 years with a mean age of approximately 59 years, while tenure of the bill's sponsor, measured by years of experience as a representative, ranges from 1 to 39 years with a mean tenure of approximately 12 years. Approximately 28 percent of the bills are sponsored by a representative whose tenure is less than 6 years and 79 percent of the bills are sponsored by a representative whose tenure is below 15 years.

The number of co-sponsors of a bill ranges between 0 and 348 with a mean of approximately 17 co-sponsors. Inspection of the distribution reveals that 60 percent of the bills are co-sponsored by fewer than 6, and 95 percent of the bills are co-sponsored by fewer than 68 members, exhibiting a large accumulation on the left tail of the distribution.

Table 6.2 Number of bills that became law tabulated by the party of the sponsor, 110th Congress

Party	Passed (%)	Failed (%)	Total
Majority (Democrat)	54 (8.50)	581 (91.50)	635
Minority (Republican)	22 (5.64)	368 (94.36)	390
Total	76	949	1025

Table 6.3 Sponsor statistics, 110th Congress

	Mean (s.d.)	Min	Max
Sponsor's age	58.99 (9.55)	34	85
Sponsor's tenure	11.85 (8.34)	1	39
Number of co-sponsors	16.59 (38.14)	0	348

Committee

When a bill is introduced in the House by a sponsor, the Speaker of the House names a committee or multiple committees to which the bill is assigned. For the 1025 observations, we collected data on the named committee, or the first named committee in the case of assignation to multiple committees. See Table 6.4.

Upon the inspection of the percentage of the bills that become law with respect to committees, bills that are referred to Oversight and Reform carry the highest pass ratio with almost 23 percent followed by Science and Technology and Natural Resources with 20 and 15 percent, respectively. Oversight and Reform bills contain a large number of simple commemorative name bills. None of the 17, 5, and 2 bills that are referred to the Administration, Budget. and Intelligence committees becomes law. The highest number of temporary bills that become law per committee are bills referred to Judiciary, and the highest number of hybrid bills that become law per committee are bills referred to Natural Resources.

6.4 FINDINGS

We have performed a binomial logistic regression to estimate the predictors of the likelihood that a bill becomes law, in which we have considered characteristics of the bill and characteristics of the sponsor of the bill as explanatory variables, as well as a set of committee dummies to measure the effect of policy domain. The results are reported in Table 6.5.

In column (1) of Table 6.5, we estimated the impact of temporary and hybrid bills versus permanent bills (Type I), on likelihood of passage with the entire sample, using only the type of bill as an explanatory factor. The results show that a non-permanent bill type exhibits a positive effect on the likelihood that a bill becomes law. In column (2), we added the real duration variable in the form of a second-order polynomial whose coefficients are significant at the conventional levels with its squared term, carrying a negative sign. The interest behind including a squared real duration variable is to examine the path of the change in likelihood that a bill becomes law with respect to increasing levels of duration and to determine whether there exists an optimal level of duration with respect to change in the likelihood of passage. The inclusion of a second-

Table 6.4 Committee statistics, 110th Congress

Committee	Referred (%)		Passed (%)		Type of Passage		
					Permanent	Temporary	Hybrid
Administration	17	(1.66)	0	(0.00)	–	–	–
Agriculture	27	(2.63)	3	(11.11)	–	1	2
Appropriations	7	(0.68)	1	(14.28)	–	–	1
Armed Services	30	(2.93)	1	(3.33)	1	–	–
Budget	5	(0.49)	0	(0.00)	–	–	–
Education and Labor	77	(7.51)	3	(3.89)	–	–	3
Energy and Commerce	147	(14.34)	9	(6.12)	5	1	3
Financial Services	53	(5.17)	4	(7.54)	3	1	–
Foreign Affairs	27	(2.63)	3	(11.11)	–	1	2
Homeland Security	14	(1.37)	2	(14.28)	–	–	2
Intelligence	2	(0.20)	0	(0.00)	–	–	–
Judiciary	107	(10.44)	9	(8.41)	3	3	3
Natural Resources	99	(9.66)	15	(15.15)	6	1	8
Oversight and Reform	48	(4.68)	11	(22.91)	11	–	–
Science and Technology	15	(1.46)	3	(20.00)	–	–	3
Small Business	8	(0.78)	1	(12.5)	–	1	–
Transportation and Infrastructure	42	(4.10)	5	(11.90)	3	2	–
Veterans Affairs	30	(2.93)	1	(3.33)	1	–	–
Ways and Means	270	(26.34)	5	(1.85)	1	1	3
Total observations	1025	(100.00)	76	(100.00)	34	12	30

order polynomial of real duration does not affect the sign or the significance of the bill type although its magnitude is slightly higher compared to its counterpart in column (1).

In column (3), we have additionally considered sponsor-related

Table 6.5 Logit estimates, 110th Congress

	(1)	(2)
Constant	−2.979*** (0.175)	−4.852*** (0.294)
Bill characteristics		
Type I	1.082*** (0.241)	1.230*** (0.276)
Type II		
Real duration		12.641*** (1.698)
Real duration squared		−10.491*** (2.246)
Sponsor characteristics		
Majority party		
Tenure		
Tenure squared		
Age		
Age squared		
Number of co-sponsors		
Number of co-sponsors squared		
Committees		
Agriculture		
Appropriations		
Armed Services		
Education and Labor		
Energy and Commerce		
Financial Services		
Foreign Affairs		
Homeland Security		
Judiciary		
Natural Resources		
Oversight and Reform		
Science and Technology		
Small Business		
Transportation and Infrastructure		
Veterans Affairs		
% correctly predicted	92.6	92.5
McFadden pseudo R-square	0.0369	0.2768
Sample size	1025	1025
Schwarz-Bayesian criterion	535.530	419.449
Log-likelihood	−260.832	−195.859
Includes tariffs and commemorative names	Yes	Yes

Notes:
Dependent variable: passage (= 1 if the bill passed, =0 otherwise).
Robust standard errors in parentheses. ***, ** and * denote statistical significance at 1%, 5% and 10% respectively.

(3)	(4)	(5)	(6)
−5.666*** (4.484)	−4.970*** (0.404)	−5.872*** (0.617)	−5.545** (0.419)
1.288*** (0.280)		1.821*** (0.321)	1.827** (0.321)
	1.487*** (0.441)		
13.968*** (1.691)	12.641** (2.080)	12.110*** (1.876)	12.956*** (1.789)
−12.421*** (2.152)	−9.882*** (2.568)	−10.163*** (2.371)	−10.978*** (2.288)
−0.167 (0.304)			
−0.038 (0.060)			
0.002 (0.001)			
0.051 (0.154)			
−0.0006 (0.0012)			
−0.010 (0.006)	−0.017** (0.008)	−0.015** (0.007)	−0.014** (0.007)
0.00006** (0.00002)	0.00007** (0.00003)	0.00009*** (0.00003)	0.00008*** (0.00003)
		0.786 (0.899)	
		1.685 (1.796)	
		0.562 (1.273)	
		0.052 (0.758)	
		1.059* (0.632)	0.624 (0.455)
		−0.515 (1.115)	
		2.151*** (0.763)	1.701*** (0.610)
		0.639 (1.196)	
		1.210* (0.635)	0.736* (0.431)
		0.810 (0.614)	
		2.391*** (0.794)	1.903*** (0.621)
		0.949 (0.815)	
		2.853*** (1.167)	2.474** (1.088)
		1.847** (0.775)	1.386** (0.630)
		0.182 (1.463)	
92.7	94.9	93.0	93.0
0.3059	0.2706	0.3468	0.3372
1025	841	957	957
452.186	292.245	484.41	427.646
−187.965	−125.919	−170.135	−172.64
Yes	No	No	No

factors, including the sponsor's age and tenure, the number of co-sponsors, and a binary variable that denotes whether or not the sponsor belongs to the majority party. The results indicate that neither sponsor age, tenure, nor party has an impact on the likelihood of passage.

In column (4), we removed hybrid bills from the sample and

considered permanent and temporary bills (Type II) only. This serves as a robustness check for the effect of permanent versus non-permanent bills on the likelihood of passage. The effect of a bill being not permanent is still significant and positive at conventional levels once the remaining explanatory factors are taken into account, and does not change after removing hybrid bills.

In columns (5) and (6), we have further considered policy domain factors as explanatory variables. There are 19 committees to which the bills in our sample are referred. However, observations from three of those committees, Administration, Budget, and Intelligence, are removed from the sample because they perfectly predict binary response failure (i.e. bills referred to those committees have never become law). This leaves 16 committees, of which the dummy variable associated with Ways and Means is identified to be highly collinear with the remaining regressors and excluded from the regression to avoid multicollinearity.[3]

The coefficient of the bill type in the last two columns remains statistically significant at conventional levels, albeit slightly higher after the inclusion of committee dummies. In column (6), we have removed the committees whose coefficients were individually and jointly statistically significantly not different from zero and reestimated the model. The results indicate the coefficients for Foreign Affairs, Judiciary, Oversight and Reform, Small Business, and Transportation and Infrastructure have statistically significant and positive impact on the likelihood that a bill becomes law. The estimates in column (6) are consistent with the previous column, although the significant and positive committee coefficients are slightly dampened after removing committees with insignificant coefficients.

---

[3] In addition to the results reported in Table 6.5, we have performed a specification analysis in which we considered additional dummy variables interacted by the type of bill and the committee dummies. Ai and Norton (2003) show that the magnitude of the interaction effect in logit does not equal the marginal effect of the interaction term. However, the computation of the interaction effect suggested by Ai and Norton may be between two continuous, two discrete, or one continuous and one discrete variable. Thus it only takes into account the incorporation of one interaction dummy variable at a time. Our preliminary estimations therefore were restricted to the estimation of only one additional interaction dummy per estimation and their effects proved to be insignificant.

The significance of the coefficients regarding bill and sponsor characteristics upon the gradual inclusion of potential explanatory factors depicts a consistent story throughout the estimations. The impact of bill type, real duration, and the number of co-sponsors are all statistically significant at conventional levels and do not change substantially after the inclusion or removal of additional factors or observations. The percentage correctly predicted by the estimations ranges from 92.5 to 94.9 percent, indicating a fairly good fit.

A particular problem with logit regression is the difficulty of interpreting the coefficients. Therefore, we have computed the response probabilities based on the last column in Table 6.5. In what follows we report the impact of non-permanence on the probability of passage as well as the partial effects of the remaining variables on the probability of passage.

When evaluating each of the continuous variables at their mean and all dummies at zero, the change in probability that a non-permanent bill becomes law is 0.0500. This impact seems relatively low, and may be partially explained by the possibility that legislators are using temporary legislation in controversial and partisan policy domains where passage probability may be low irrespective of timing rule. In addition, legislators may be using temporal restrictions to increase the number of votes they receive in an election. By passing a series of temporary bills, legislators can increase the visibility of a particular issue that may be important to their supporters. To the extent that the temporary legislation benefits a legislator from increased visibility, temporal restrictions may have less impact when the opposing legislator symmetrically benefits from opposing that legislation – irrespective of its temporary or permanent status.

Since the effect of bill type on the likelihood of passage depends on the values chosen for the remaining (continuous) variables, we further report the change in probability that a non-permanent bill becomes law at various levels of real duration while evaluating the number of co-sponsors at mean and all committee dummies at zero, which is depicted in Figure 6.1.

From Figure 6.1 if 20 percent of the maximum possible duration is consumed for deliberation over a non-permanent bill, i.e real duration equals 0.2, the probability that this non-permanent bill becomes law is higher by approximately 0.13. Similarly, at a real duration level of 0.6, this probability is even higher by approximately 0.36. This level yields the maximal change in passage probability.

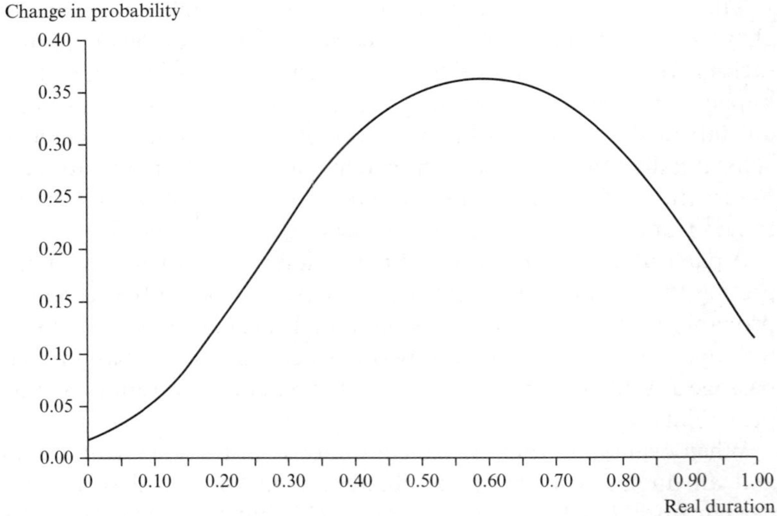

Note: The number of co-sponsors and its squared term are evaluated at their means. All committee dummies are evaluated at 0.

Figure 6.1 The effect of non-permanence on the probability of passage at various levels of real duration

Figure 6.2 displays the partial effect of real duration on the probability that a bill becomes law. Our particular interest is to determine whether there exists an optimal level of duration with respect to change in the likelihood that a bill becomes law. In Figure 6.2, the effect of real duration for a non-permanent bill is given on the left y-axis and the effect of real duration for a permanent bill is given on the right y-axis. Marginal increases in the levels of real duration increase the probability that a bill becomes law both for permanent and non-permanent bills, however, the magnitude of the increase in this probability is much higher for non-permanent bills. The change in the probability that a bill becomes law is maximized, and this probability is higher by about 1.3 for non-permanent bills at a duration level such that only 30 percent of the maximum possible duration is consumed and higher by about 0.38 for permanent bills at a duration level such that only 35 percent of the maximum possible duration is consumed. The change in the probability that a permanent or a non-permanent bill becomes law is still positive but

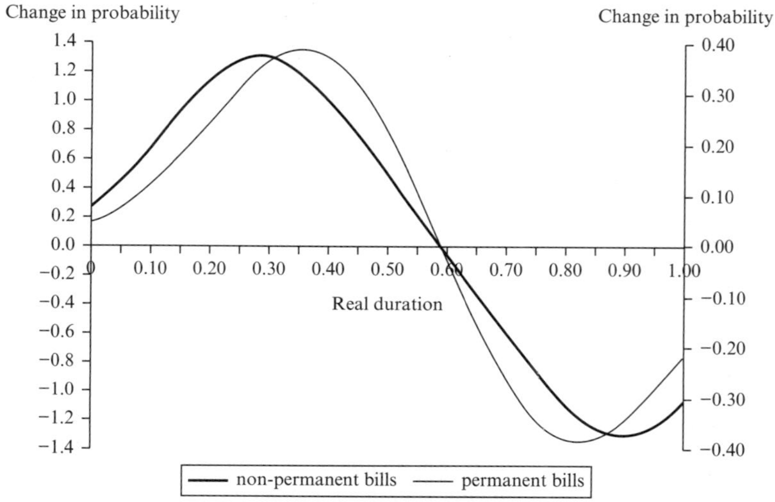

Note: The number of co-sponsors and its squared term are evaluated at their means. All committee dummies are evaluated at 0. Non-permanent bills read on the left y-axis and permanent bills read on the right y-axis.

Figure 6.2 The effect of real duration on the probability of passage

decreasing beyond optimal levels of real duration up to a real duration level of about 0.60. At the given value of the remaining explanatory variables and starting at a real duration level of 0.60, a small increase in real duration lowers the probability that a bill becomes law by about 0.03 and 0.05 for permanent and non-permanent bills respectively.

The approximate change in probability that a non-permanent bill becomes law with different numbers of co-sponsors is depicted in Figure 6.3. If there are no co-sponsors for a non-permanent bill, the probability that this bill becomes law, given that real duration is fixed at its mean, is higher by approximately 0.06. If there are 100 co-sponsors for a non-permanent bill, the probability that it becomes law is higher by only 0.028. From Figure 6.3, the partial effect of a non-permanent bill on the change in the likelihood of passage is low if the number of co-sponsors is evaluated at a value below circa 150 members. When co-sponsors exceed 150, the partial effect of the non-permanent type is increasing, up to 320 co-sponsors.

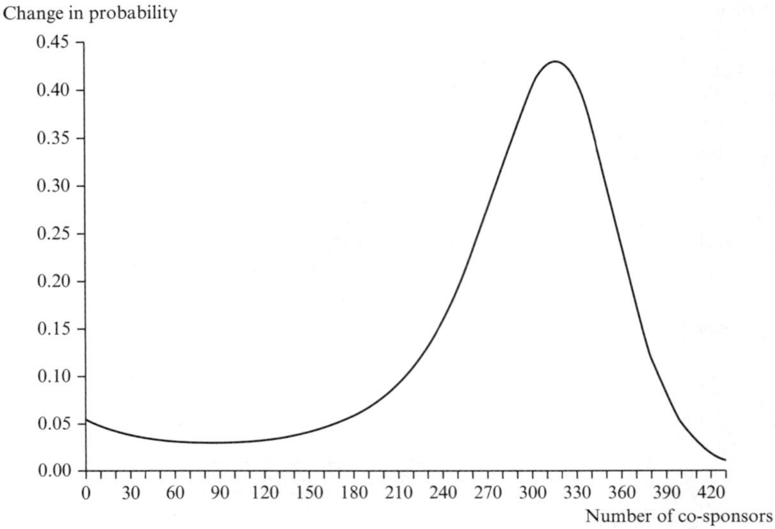

Note: The real duration and its squared term are evaluated at their means. All committee dummies are evaluated at 0.

Figure 6.3 The effect of non-permanence on the probability of passage with varying number of co-sponsors

The path of the effect of the number of co-sponsors on the probability that a bill becomes law is given in Figure 6.4. An additional co-sponsor up to 100 co-sponsors does not exhibit a significantly higher probability that a bill becomes law both for permanent and non-permanent bills. The optimal number of co-sponsors for a non-permanent bill is around 300 representatives, such that the probability that a non-permanent bill becomes law is higher by about 0.0082 for an additional co-sponsor at this level. However, the optimal number of co-sponsors for a permanent bill is much higher, around 340 co-sponsors, such that the probability that a permanent bill becomes law is higher by about 0.0123 for an additional co-sponsor at this level, indicating that non-permanent bills require a smaller number of co-sponsors than permanent bills to yield the maximal change in the probability of passage. Overall, the partial impact of the number of co-sponsors on the probability of passage is very small.

We have depicted in Figure 6.5 the partial effects of the committees

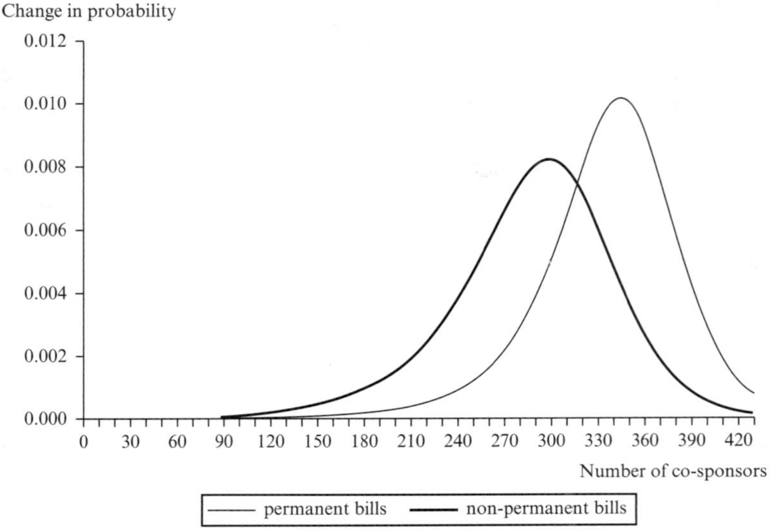

Note: The real duration and its squared term are evaluated at their means. All committee dummies are evaluated at 0.

Figure 6.4 The effect of the number of co-sponsors on the probability of passage

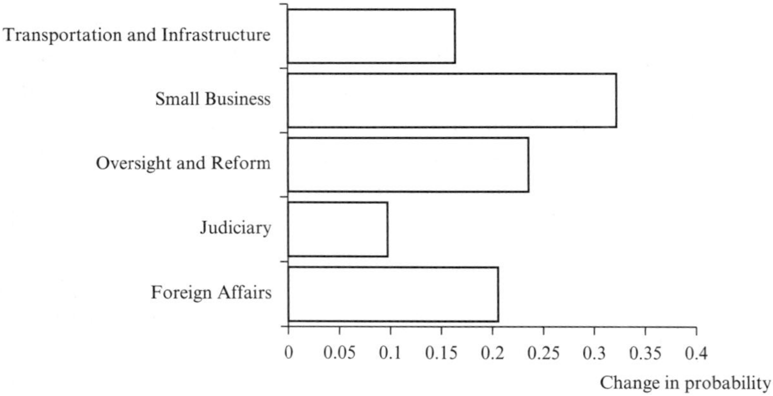

Figure 6.5 The effect of a non-permanent bill on the probability of passage within committees

on the likelihood that a non-permanent bill becomes law, depending on the committee to which it is referred. Consider two bills, one permanent and the other non-permanent, both referred to the same committee. If both are referred to Foreign Affairs, the change in probability that the non-permanent bill becomes law is higher by about 0.206 compared to the permanent bill referred to the same committee. We found that the change in the likelihood that a non-permanent bill becomes law within a particular committee ranges between 0.097 and 0.323.

6.5 CONCLUSION

We attempt to measure the impact of temporary provisions on the probability of bill passage using data from the 110th Congress on bill characteristics, sponsor characteristics, and binary information on committees to which the bill is assigned. Our study imposes several limitations. If legislators trade off temporal restrictions against the substance of the legislation, this suggests either that a temporal restriction is determined by the legislator's anticipation of whether the bill would pass or not (i.e. its expected passage) or that a temporal restriction is correlated with some unobserved or non-measurable characteristic of the bill (e.g. the degree of controversy in its substantive provisions). Although we attempted to address some of these issues by controlling for the committee to which the bill is assigned, both scenarios are bound to lead to an endogeneity problem. In this case, one should apply nonlinear instrumental variable estimation methods. We certainly do not rule out endogeneity. However, the difficulty with an instrumental variable framework is the identification of valid instruments. In our case, this translates into finding at least one instrument that is uncorrelated with unobservable confounder variables, that is sufficiently correlated with the type of bill, and that can neither have a direct influence on passage nor be correlated with the error term of our model. Given the data we believe that such an instrument does not exist. Therefore, our results should be treated with caution.

Although temporary and permanent legislation can govern for the same length of time with extensions or repeals, the probability that non-permanent legislation becomes law is higher by about 0.05. The optimal duration for deliberation is less for non-permanent bills, as is the optimal number of co-sponsors. That non-permanent legislation is more likely to become law than permanent legislation supports the claim that non-permanent legislation incurs lower transactions cost. When there is no probability of repeal or extension, permanent bills default to an infinite stream of benefits and non-permanent bills default to a finite stream of benefits. If legislators are paying for legislation in benefits, then non-permanent bills should pass more easily. When the probability of rescission is 1, non-permanent bills are less costly because they expire by default. When there is no probability of repeal and the probability of extension is 1, non-permanent bills are less costly only in favorable legislative environments, i.e. where legislation costs are decreasing. Interestingly, non-permanent bills that originate in Foreign Affairs, Judiciary, Oversight and Reform, Small Business, and Transportation and Infrastructure are more likely to become law than permanent bills in those same committees by about 0.21, 0.10, 0.23, 0.32, and 0.16, respectively. This suggests that those committees provide favorable environments for temporary policies, and that the optimal choice of timing rule may vary with policy domain.

7. Sponsor's age

7.1 INTRODUCTION

As we have seen in the previous chapter, non-permanent legislation is more likely to become law than permanent legislation, a proxy for incurring comparatively lower transactions cost for its passage. Legislators, especially older legislators nearing retirement, would presumably prefer lower-cost temporary legislation if they receive compliance benefits for a shorter time and smaller magnitude. Instead, if they prefer higher-cost permanent legislation, they may receive an immediate transfer from interest groups of sufficient magnitude, or a further benefit from legislating compliance outcomes beyond their tenure, which we refer to as a legacy benefit. To the extent that permanent legislation increases total compliance over time, legislators who pay for legacy benefits may prefer to incur additional costs for its passage, even when the alternative cost structure of temporary legislation provides transactions cost savings in the short to medium term.[1] In order to test this theory, we test for a causal relationship between the selection of a permanent timing rule and the age of the bill's sponsor.

This is accomplished by performing a binomial logistic regression to estimate the predictors of the likelihood that a permanent provision is included in a bill, in which we consider characteristics of the bill and characteristics of the bill's sponsor (including age) as explanatory variables. Thus the age of the bill's sponsor is a measure for the legislator's willingness to pay for a legacy benefit, where older legislators are willing to pay more. Holding the other regressors fixed, if increases in sponsor's age explain the inclusion of permanent provisions, then older legislators receive either immediate transfers from lobbies, legacy benefits or some mixture of the two. The legacy claim is qualified as a possible mixture of transfer and legacy benefits

[1] See chapter 3.

because the data does not permit the use of the former as an explanatory variable. Nonetheless, if the assumption is made that older legislators have sufficiently high discount rates for lobby transfers (in particular when nearing the end of their lives), or that the transfers are sufficiently small, then the existence of a causal relationship between age and the selection of a permanent provision may provide evidence that legislators receive benefits from compliance outcomes that occur beyond their tenure.

7.2 THEORY

Consider a legislative benefit function:

$$\beta(\tau, \bar{d}, a_0) = -y(\tau) - v(\tau, \bar{d})^2 + h(\tau, \bar{d}, a_0)$$

where y and v are the fixed and marginal costs of legislating compliance and h are legacy benefits. The timing rule $\tau \in \{0, 1\}$ represents the legislator's binary decision to legislate permanently or temporarily. Recall that legislators minimize transactions cost by choosing τ in response to aggregate compliance $\bar{d}$ (chapter 2, section 2.2.3). Their choice of τ, given aggregate compliance $\bar{d}$ minimizes compliance costs v, which they incur during their tenure as legislators. Proposition 3 shows that when aggregate compliance is increasing, and fixed costs y are sufficiently low, temporary legislation minimizes total legislation costs.

We now introduce a further term h, which represents a legacy benefit from legislating compliance outcomes that occur beyond the legislator's tenure. When there is no probability of extension or repeal, legacy benefits $h(0) < h(1)$ since temporary legislation provides a discrete stream of benefits and permanent legislation provides an infinite stream of benefits. Instead, when there is some probability of extension or repeal, legacy benefits depend on the product of the aggregate compliance level $\bar{d}$ in each legislative period and the legislative period lengths. Assuming that the length under a permanent timing rule is greater than the length under a temporary timing rule, $h(0) < h(1)$. Legacy benefits further depend on the exogenously determined age of the legislator a_0 where $\frac{\delta h}{\delta a_0} > 1$. That older legislators experience greater legacy benefits rests on the assumptions that legislators value passing legislation that remains in effect, and that older legislators have decreasing opportunities to do so. Younger legislators have a larger portion of their careers in front of them, and have more time to legislate compliance outcomes that occur after their tenure. Thus they discount permanent legislation to a greater extent then older legislators. Choosing permanent legislation maximizes legacy benefits unequivocally, but those benefits may be offset by permanent legislation's higher cost if $\bar{d}$ is sufficiently increasing and temporary fixed costs y are sufficiently low.

Because older legislators value legacy benefits to a greater extent than younger legislators, they differ in their valuation of sufficient $\bar{d}$ and y. Aggregate compliance must be higher and temporary fixed costs must be lower in order for older legislators to optimally choose a temporary timing rule. They have fewer opportunities to legislate compliance outcomes and therefore value legislation that governs for a greater length of time. When a_0 is sufficiently high, their legacy benefits outweigh any transactions cost savings that may be available under a temporary timing rule. We test this theory by performing a binomial logistic regression to estimate the predictors of the likelihood that a permanent provision is included in a bill, in which we consider characteristics of the bill's sponsor (including age) and characteristics of the bill as explanatory variables.

7.3 DATA AND SUMMARY STATISTICS

Chapter 6 section 6.3 above provides descriptive information of the data. Additional summary statistics regarding bill and sponsor characteristics are reported below.

Bill characteristics

Out of the randomly sampled 1025 bills, 703 (68.59 percent) are permanent and 322 (31.41 percent) are non-permanent. Of the

Table 7.1 Bills tabulated by type, 110th Congress

Type	Total (%)	Passed (%)
Permanent	703 (68.59)	34 (4.84)
Non-permanent	322 (31.41)	42 (13.04)
Total	1025 (100.00)	76 (7.42)

703 permanent bills, 34 (4.84 percent) become law. Of the 322 non-permanent bills, 42 (13.04 percent) become law.

Sponsor characteristics

Each bill is sponsored by a legislator and can be co-sponsored by any additional number of the remaining 434 members of the House of Representatives. For each observation, we collected information on the age of the sponsor, the party of the sponsor and the number of co-sponsors. We report the mean and relative frequency of the sponsor's age for permanent and non-permanent bills, for bills that become law, and for bills sponsored by a member of the majority party. Additionally, we report summary information on the relationship between real duration and sponsor's age as well as co-sponsors and sponsor's age.

Figure 7.1 displays the relative frequency of the sponsor's age, irrespective of bill type. The mean sponsor age is 58.994 with a standard deviation of 9.559 years. The maximum relative frequency is 62 years. Figures 7.2 and 7.3 display the relative frequencies of sponsor's age for permanent and non-permanent bills. The mean sponsor age for permanent bills is 58.762 with a standard deviation of 9.712 years. The highest relative frequency is 62 years. The

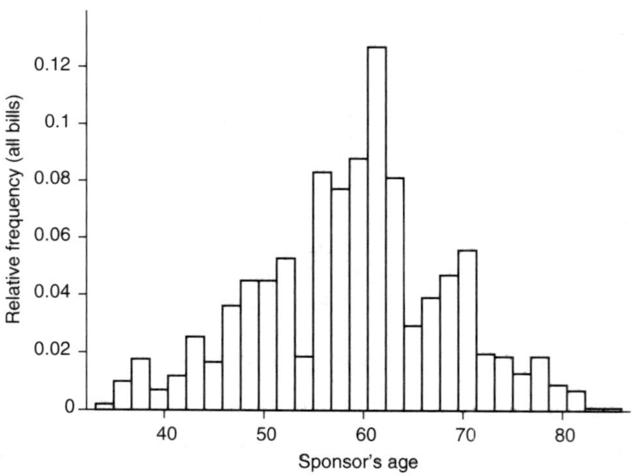

Figure 7.1 Relative frequency of sponsor's age, N = 1025, 110th Congress

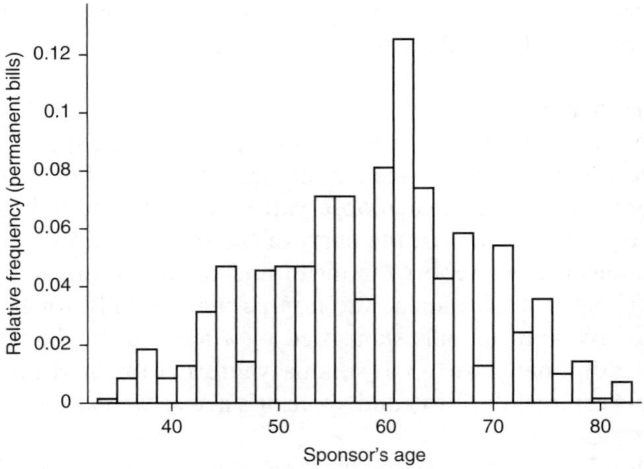

Figure 7.2 Relative frequency of sponsor's age, N = 703, 110th Congress

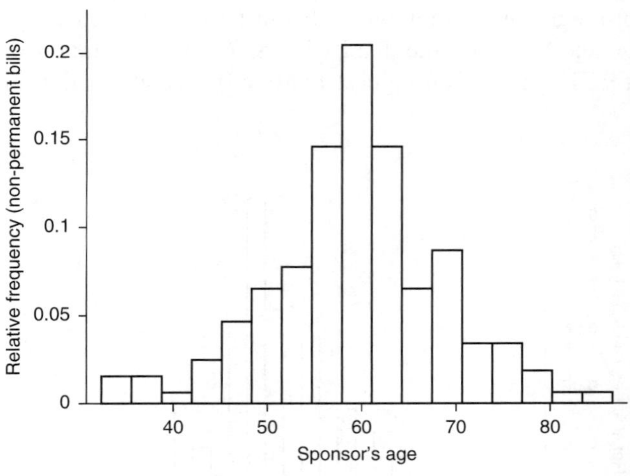

Figure 7.3 Relative frequency of sponsor's age, N = 322, 110th Congress

mean sponsor age for non-permanent bills is 59.500 with a standard deviation of 9.212 years. The highest relative frequency is 59 years.

Figure 7.4 displays the relative frequency of the sponsor's age for all bills that become law. The mean sponsor age for all passed bills

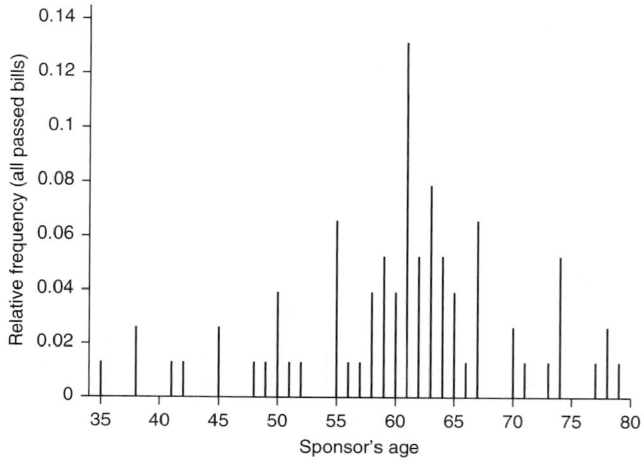

Figure 7.4 Relative frequency of sponsor's age, N = 76, 110th Congress

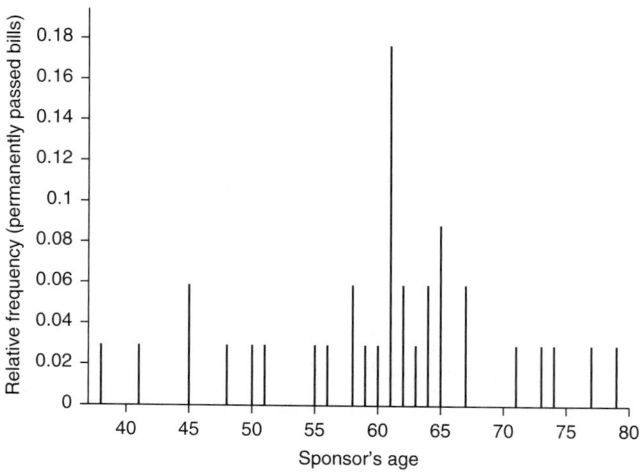

Figure 7.5 Relative frequency of sponsor's age, N = 34, 110th Congress

is 60.421 with a standard deviation of 9.425. The maximum relative frequency is 61 years. Figures 7.5 and 7.6 display the relative frequency of the sponsor's age for permanent and non-permanent bills that become law. Their mean sponsor's ages are 60.235 with a

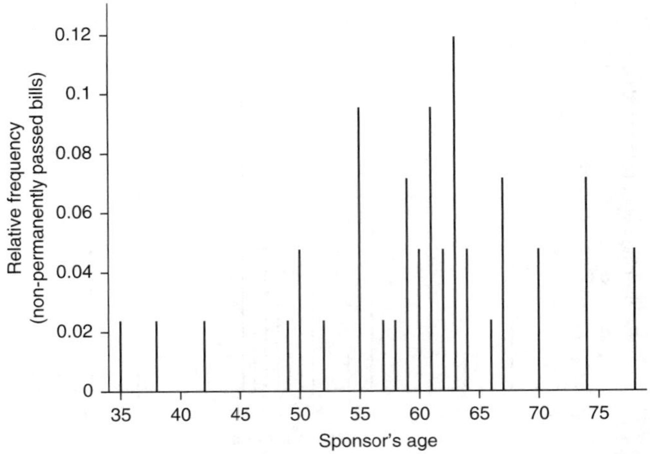

Figure 7.6 Relative frequency of sponsor's age, N = 42, 110th Congress

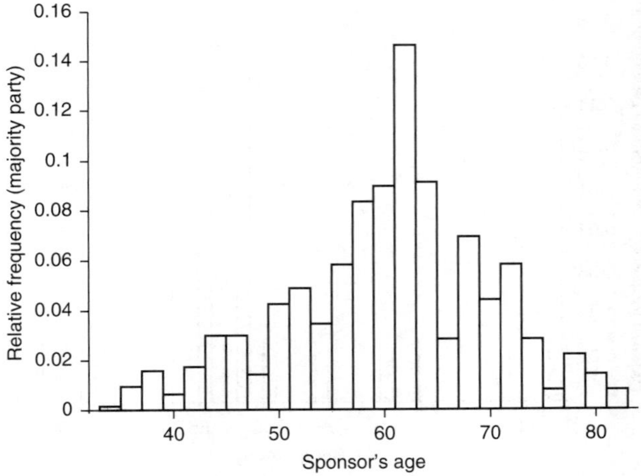

Figure 7.7 Relative frequency of sponsor's age, N = 635, 110th Congress

standard deviation of 9.586 years, and 60.571 with a standard deviation of 9.407 years. Their maximum relative frequencies are 61 and 63 years.

Figure 7.7 displays the relative frequency of the sponsor's age for

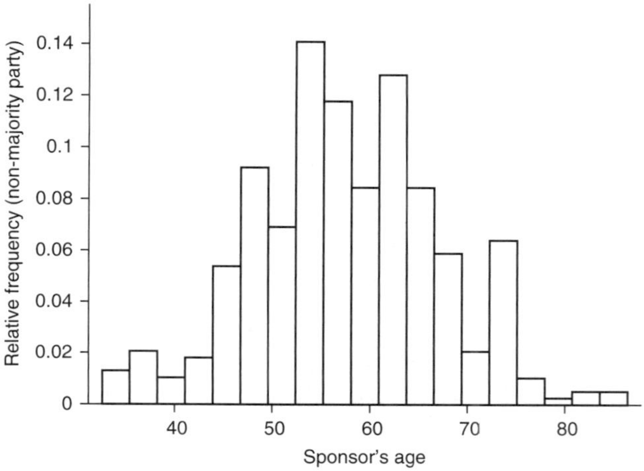

Figure 7.8 Relative frequency of sponsor's age, N = 390, 110th Congress

bills sponsored by a member of the majority party. The mean sponsor age for majority-party bills is 59.833 with a standard deviation of 9.581 years. The highest relative frequency is 62 years. Figure 7.8 displays the relative frequency of the sponsor's age for bills not sponsored by a member of the majority party. The mean sponsor age is slightly lower at 57.628 with a standard deviation of 9.376 years. The maximum relative frequency is 54 years. Figure 7.9 plots real duration against sponsor's age and provides a least squares fit. For every additional year of sponsor's age, real duration increases by 0.00177. Figure 7.10 plots the number of co-sponsors against sponsor's age, again providing a least squares fit. For each additional year of sponsor's age, the number of co-sponsors increases by 0.326.

Committee

Table 7.2 reports the descriptive statistics of the sponsor's age tabulated by committee and bill type. The age of a bill's sponsor in all committees ranges between 34 and 82 years with a mean age of approximately 59 years for permanent legislation, and ranges between 34 and 85 years with approximately the same mean age for non-permanent legislation.

For permanent legislation, the Armed Services committee has the highest mean age (61.82 years) and the Intelligence committee

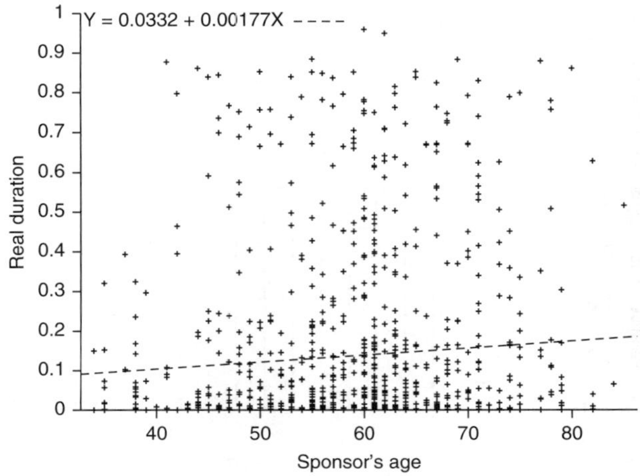

Figure 7.9 *Real duration plotted against sponsor's age with least squares fit, 110th Congress*

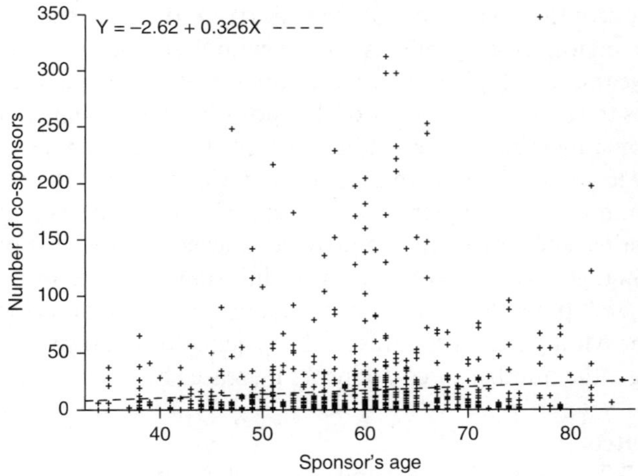

Figure 7.10 *Co-sponsors plotted against sponsor's age with least squares fit, 110th Congress*

has the lowest mean age (52.00 years). For non-permanent legislation, the Oversight and Reform committee has the highest mean age (67.33 years) and the Armed Services committee has the lowest mean age (53.50 years).

Table 7.2 *Descriptive statistics of sponsor's age, tabulated by committee and bill type, 110th Congress*

Committee	Permanent				Non-permanent			
	Referred (%)	Mean age (s.d.)	Min	Max	Referred (%)	Mean age (s.d.)	Min	Max
Administration	14	56.71 (8.53)	45	71	3	64.00 (6.00)	58	70
Agriculture	15	54.20 (10.96)	37	71	12	58.00 (12.11)	34	74
Appropriations	3	52.33 (1.15)	51	53	4	63.50 (6.46)	57	70
Armed Services	28	61.82 (8.24)	45	78	2	53.50 (3.56)	51	56
Budget	4	56.75 (12.29)	39	65	1	55.00 (0.00)	55	55
Education and Labor	47	61.66 (9.21)	34	79	30	58.70 (8.41)	34	71
Energy and Commerce	104	59.33 (9.64)	38	82	43	58.84 (8.64)	41	82
Financial Services	44	59.48 (8.57)	44	77	9	65.56 (5.81)	55	71
Foreign Affairs	23	59.74 (10.06)	38	78	4	66.25 (6.99)	57	74
Homeland Security	9	55.79 (11.35)	44	79	5	61.40 (14.01)	49	85
Intelligence	2	52 (11.31)	44	60	0	–	–	–
Judiciary	84	58.36 (9.26)	35	79	23	60.39 (6.66)	48	79
Natural Resources	73	60.16 (9.71)	35	79	26	60.62 (8.41)	46	84
Oversight and Reform	45	57.71 (9.87)	38	80	3	67.33 (3.79)	63	70
Science and Technology	4	62.50 (9.00)	55	73	11	57.55 (10.78)	38	74
Small Business	6	57.83 (3.13)	55	64	2	55 (0.00)	55	55
Transportation and Infrastructure	35	60.86 (10.18)	35	78	7	62.86 (9.32)	53	74
Veterans Affairs	28	56.11 (10.02)	35	73	2	56.50 (6.36)	52	61
Ways and Means	135	57.28 (10.30)	35	82	135	58.81 (9.94)	35	82
Total Observations	703	58.76 (9.71)	34	82	322	59.50 (9.21)	34	85

7.4 FINDINGS

We have performed a binomial logistic regression to estimate the predictors of the likelihood that a bill is permanent, in which we have considered the characteristics of the sponsor of the bill and the characteristics of the bill itself, as explanatory variables. The set of committee dummies is used to restrict the sample.

In column (1) of table 7.3, we estimated the impact of the log of age on the likelihood that a bill is permanent with the entire sample, using only log of age as an explanatory factor. The results show that

Table 7.3 Logit estimates, 110th Congress

	(1)	(2)	(3)	(4)
Constant	2.656 (1.628)	−6.172 (4.068)	−6.610 (4.531)	−6.414 (4.403)
Log of age	−1.062 (0.920)	3.952* (2.294)	4.810* (2.588)	4.625* (2.577)
Passed			−1.561** (0.691)	−1.502** (0.640)
Majority party			−1.087** (0.452)	−1.141*** (0.434)
Number of co-sponsors			−0.016 (0.011)	
Number of co-sponsors squared			9.091 (0.00001)	
Real duration			2.332 (2.677)	
Real duration squared			−3.844 (3.483)	
% correctly predicted	68.6%	69.2%	72.1%	72.1%
McFadden pseudo R-square	0.001	0.013	0.101	0.091
Sample size	1025	172	172	172
Schwarz-Bayesian criterion	1287.66	218.316	229.246	212.232
Log-likelihood	−636.90	−104.011	−94.033	−95.821
Restricts committees	No	Yes	Yes	Yes

Notes:
Dependent variable: permanent (= 1 if the bill is permanent, =0 otherwise).
Robust standard errors in parentheses. ***, ** and * denote statistical significance at 1%, 5% and 10% respectively.

the log of age does not exhibit an effect on the likelihood that a bill is permanent. We then restricted the sample to each committee individually, again estimating the impact of log of age on the likelihood that a bill is permanent. The estimation in column (2) comprises those committees where the log of age significantly affects the likelihood that a bill is permanent. When restricting the sample to the committees of Armed Services, Education and Labor, Small Business, Science and Technology, and Transportation and Infrastructure, log of age exhibits a significant and positive effect on the likelihood that a bill is permanent.

In column (3), we added the remaining bill and sponsor characteristics. The results show that bills that are passed and bills that are sponsored by a member of the majority party significantly and negatively impact the likelihood that a bill is permanent. The number of co-sponsors, the number of co-sponsors squared and real duration and real duration squared are not significant. We removed those factors and reestimated the restricted sample in column (4). The coefficients of log of age, passed, and majority party remain statistically significant at conventional levels. The percentage correctly predicted by the estimations ranges from 68.6 to 72.1 percent, indicating a moderate fit.

As in the previous chapter, we have computed the marginal effects of the significant variables using the final estimation in Table 7.3. When evaluating the passed and majority-party dummies at zero, a 0.940 percentage increase in sponsor age increases the likelihood that a bill is permanent by 4.625 percent. When evaluating the log of age at its mean and the majority party dummy at 0, a bill that is passed, instead of not passed, decreases the probability that a bill is permanent by 0.352. When evaluating the log of age at its mean and the passed dummy at 0, being sponsored by the majority party decreases the probability that a bill is permanent by 0.210.

7.5 CONCLUSION

There are several reasons why the findings might only moderately support the theory that older legislators prefer permanent legislation. First, the explanatory factor of interest, sponsor's age, may be biased. Sponsors of legislation may not adequately represent the legislators as an entire group and further study might include the age of each legislator who voted for each bill, or some other measure of the relationship between bill and age as an explanatory factor. Second, the regression may prove more robust when controlling for interest group contributions. Since data on contributions to individual bills does not exist, an index might be constructed that provides relative values between groups of bills based upon some theory. For example, bills originating in the Agriculture committee and sponsored by legislators from Illinois might be expected to exhibit higher levels of contributions than bills originating in the Veterans Affairs committee and sponsored by legislators from New Mexico. Future work might include some type of composite measure along these lines as an explanatory factor. Nonetheless, these results do show a significant effect of sponsor's age on the selection of timing rule. Bills originating within the committees of Armed Services, Education and Labor, Small Business, Science and Technology, and Transportation and Infrastructure, are 4.625 percent more likely to be permanent when the sponsor's age is increased by 0.940 percent.

8. Conclusion

The choice of temporary versus permanent legislation is strategic. This is a reflection of the interdependencies between the legislature and citizens, the legislature and a lobby, and a current legislature and a future legislature. In each relationship, the legislature's decision to legislate temporarily or permanently depends on the action chosen by the other group. The strategic problem arises because the group's choice of action is not independent; it is affected by the legislature's choice of timing rule. Throughout this book, an action chosen by citizens, a lobby, or a future legislature has been conceptualized as a potential benefit that accrues to the legislature. It has taken the form of increased citizen compliance, revealed lobby information, and reduced political opponent popularity. In exchange for the benefit, the legislature pays a cost, i.e. the transactions cost of either temporary or permanent legislation. Here lies the opportunity for the legislature. Because each type of legislation allocates costs to different points in time, the legislature can wait for something favorable to happen before incurring the full cost of the legislation. In the case of an interaction with citizens, the legislature can wait for the law to manifest an update in normative behavior or citizen organization. In the case of an interaction with a lobby, the legislature can wait for the law to induce information revelation. And in the case of an interaction with a future legislature, the current legislature can wait for the law to reduce an opponent's popularity. Each of these benefits may not have occurred given a permanent enactment, or even if they did occur, they may not have been possible to accrue unless paid for with a temporary legislation cost structure. A summary of the key findings may be useful at this point.

With respect to the interactions between the legislature and citizens and the legislature and a lobby, there exist possibilities for joint maximization since the legislature's gain is not necessarily the citizens' or lobby's loss. Citizens desire legislation that comports to their actions, and to the extent that new legislation causes them to reveal their actions to the legislature, legislation can be adjusted to satisfy their newly revealed preference. When temporary legislation is less costly to adjust than permanent legislation, its choice can maximize social welfare. The conclusion that we draw in proposition 3 is that when citizens are moving their social actions toward regulated behavior in new legislation, social welfare is maximized with a temporary timing rule. This is subject to the qualification that the cost savings due to the expressive effect must outweigh the difference in temporary and permanent enactment costs plus any fixed costs associated with each temporary extension. The same logic applies to the legislature–lobby relationship. Social welfare may be maximized with a temporary timing rule when lobbies reveal information that leads to a favorable adjustment to the legislation. Even when adjustment is unfavorable, social welfare may be maximized still, if lobbies receive sufficient reputation benefits for revealing (proposition 7). A temporary enactment is particularly important in this scenario because it signals to the lobby that legislators are committed to the policy. Committed legislators who know that the lobby will reveal information in exchange for reputation benefits demonstrate their commitment by legislating temporarily. This is because adjusting temporary legislation is less costly then adjusting permanent legislation. If cost-minimizing legislators had sent a permanent enactment signal, lobbies would know that no adjustment is in sight (lemma 5).

For more or less opposite reasons, permanent legislation maximizes social welfare. As shown in proposition 1, when citizens are not moving their social actions toward regulated behavior in new legislation, that is, the legislation is not creating beneficial residual effects like legal expression, permanent legislation avoids the additional transactions cost imposed by multiple extensions of temporary legislation. Social cost is likely to be minimized with a permanent timing rule because the legislation governs permanently without further (costly) legislative action. Likewise, permanent legislation maximizes social welfare in the legislature–lobby relationship when the legislature is less committed to policy precision and does not value adjustment significantly. Its low valuation of adjustment, coupled with a lobby's low valuation of adjustment and reputation benefits, are concerns that render a choice of permanent legislation socially optimal (proposition 6).

The theoretical conclusions discussed above are conceived in a transactions cost framework characterized as short to medium term. This is to distinguish them from longer-term considerations that often escape the objective functions of legislators employed in similar analyses, which are instead dominated by material considerations such as campaign contributions and other like benefits. In addition to short- to medium-term compliance benefits, chapter 3 supposes that legislators benefit from extending normative influence beyond their careers, or even their lifetimes. We consider their normative influence at various points in time (sections 3.3.1–3.3.3). At the furthest point, normative compliance occurs involuntarily. Involuntary compliance with social norms moves in uncharted waters for law and economics, and we go to considerable length to show that it can occur inside a rational-choice framework. The key is that first- and second-party enforcement are understood to be felt in relation to behavioral alternatives. When the alternatives are forgotten, pride and guilt can lose their meaning, and normative compliance can appear without aim. The compliance is still rooted in an earlier entrepreneurial investment in social norms, however, and the rational-choice framework thus remains intact. Chapter 3 underscores the importance of the interrelation between entrepreneurial investment in social norms and the decision to legislate temporarily or permanently. Older legislators nearing retirement may push for costly permanent bills when they could otherwise minimize transactions cost with temporary bills. Their benefit is that they increase the likelihood of leaving a normative legacy embodied in the legislation, which can leave a normative influence that varies in intensity according to the level of their normative investment.

Instead, temporary taxation can be used as a short-term strategy for reelection. Because most temporary taxation expires during an election year, current legislators force future legislators to incur political costs that can cost them an election by either extending or failing to extend tax legislation. Current legislators avoid paying immediate political costs for passing temporary taxation by circumventing offset requirements. In addition, passage of temporary tax cuts or spending increases that are paid for at a future point in time incur debt service costs that are externalized onto the public. A constitutional stipulation that temporary tax cuts or spending increases and their offsets be realized immediately forces legislators to internalize both political costs and debt servicing costs, and exerts a downward pressure on using temporary tax legislation as a reelection strategy.

Part II examines these theoretical concerns empirically. Of critical importance is the measurement of the transactions cost of temporary legislation in relation to the transactions cost of permanent legislation. Our first theoretical conclusion regarding the socially optimal use of temporary legislation when law leaves residual effects is subject to the qualification that any cost savings due to those effects must outweigh the difference in temporary and permanent enactment costs. The empirical analysis in chapter 6 addresses this qualification. We examine the relationship between temporal restriction and passage probability. The likelihood that a bill becomes law is a metric for transactions cost, and each predictor of likelihood is understood as a contributory factor of cost. The analysis shows that non-permanent bills are more likely to become law than permanent bills by about 0.05, implying that the transactions cost of passing non-permanent bills is lower than the transactions cost of passing permanent bills. Proposition 3 is probed further, in that we examine the partial effects of legislative committee on the likelihood that a non-permanent bill becomes law, depending upon the committee to which the bill is referred. Committee is a metric for policy domain, and our interest here is to see whether some policy domains are more favorable for temporary legislation than others. This question is directly related to proposition 3 when we assume that some legislative committees deliberate legislation that is more likely to leave residual effects. We find that non-permanent legislation referred to Foreign Affairs, Judiciary, Oversight and Reform, Small Business, and Transportation and Infrastructure is more likely to become law than permanent legislation referred to those same committees by about 0.21, 0.10, 0.23, 0.32, and 0.16, respectively. While the interaction between the substantive provisions and temporal restrictions of the legislation may confound the results, our model formalizes the intuition that temporary legislation passes more easily than permanent legislation, and importantly, demonstrates that the optimal choice of temporary or permanent legislation may vary with policy domain.

Chapter 7 turns to the question of statutory and normative legacies. According to the short- to medium-term transactions cost framework laid out in chapter 3, older legislators nearing retirement might be expected to sponsor a disproportionate amount of temporary legislation. Why incur higher permanent legislation costs for compliance benefits that occur beyond their tenure? While immediate interest-group transfers might explain the choice of permanent legislation in some instances, legacy benefits might explain the choice in others. The empirical analysis in chapter 7 does not separate these factors, and leaves the question open for future study. What it does establish, however, is that sponsor age is a predictor of the likelihood that a bill is permanent. When legislation is referred to the committees of Armed Services, Education and Labor, Small Business, Science and Technology, and Transportation and Infrastructure (collectively), a 0.940 percent increase in the sponsor's age increases the likelihood that the bill is permanent by 4.625 percent. This suggests that legislators are willing to incur additional costs in order to legislate compliance beyond their tenure, even when faced with a potentially lower cost alternative of legislating temporarily.

This book has sought to show that the choice of temporary versus permanent legislation is strategic. It has clarified the conditions for either choice to maximize social welfare, especially with respect to interactions between the legislature and citizens, and the legislature and a lobby. Temporary legislation permits a further degree of flexibility in statutory lawmaking, which can allow society to benefit from the good things that happen after an enactment. The law can be expressive, or a lobby can reveal information. Sometimes those things do not happen, and permanent legislation may be a socially better choice. One of the important questions that remains is how the use of temporary legislation has changed over time. Data is available for prior sessions of Congress at least back to 1973 (the 93rd Congress). Time-series data can answer questions regarding how the use of temporary legislation differs before, during, and after the peak of the sunset movement. It can also shed light on the changing magnitudes of opposition within various policy domains, which may be of importance for developing a more nuanced theory regarding the role of temporary legislation in the strategic interaction between legislatures and citizens.

Bibliography

Abel, A. B. (1983). Optimal investment under uncertainity. *American Economic Review*, 73: 228.

Ai, C. and Norton, E. C. (2003). Interaction terms in logit and probit models. *Economics Letters*, 80: 123–9.

Anderson, S. (2008). Practical and nonpractical guilt. In *Conference – Emotion in Context: Exploring the Interaction between Emotions and Legal Institutions*. University of Chicago Law School.

Auerbach, A. J. (2006). Budget windows, sunsets, and fiscal control. *Journal of Public Economics*, 90: 87–100.

Becker, G. S. (1996a). Habits, addictions, and traditions. In *Accounting for Tastes*, chapter 6, pages 119–35. Harvard University Press, Cambridge, MA, USA.

Becker, G. S. (1996b). A theory of social interactions. In *Accounting for Tastes*, chapter 8, pages 162–94. Harvard University Press, Cambridge, MA, USA.

Benaim, M. and Weibull, J. W. (2003). Deterministic approximation of stochastic evolution in games. *Econometrica*, 71: 873–903.

Benson, B. (1990). *The Enterprise of Law*. Pacific Research Institute for Public Policy, San Francisco.

Bikhchandani, S., Hirshleifer, D., and Welch, I. (1992). A theory of fads, fashion, custom, and cultural change as informational cascades. *The Journal of Political Economy*, 100(5): 992–1026.

Binmore, K. (1992). *Fun and Games*. D.C. Heath, Lexington, MA, USA.

Binmore, K. and Samuelson, L. (1997). Muddling through: noisy equilibrium selection. *Journal of Economic Theory*, 74: 235–65.

Buchanan, J. (1975). *Limits of Liberty: Between Anarchy and Leviathan*. University of Chicago Press, Chicago.

Calabresi, G. (1982). *A Common Law for the Age of Statutes*. Harvard University Press, Cambridge, MA, USA.

Carbonara, E., Parisi, F., and von Wangenheim, G. (2008). Lawmakers as norm entrepreneurs. *Review of Law and Economics*, 4: 779–99.

Coglianese, C., Zeckhauser, R., and Parson, E. (2004). Seeking truth for power: Informational strategy and regulatory policy making. *Minnesota Law Review*, 89: 277.

Cooter, R. (1998). Expressive law and economics. *Journal of Legal Studies*, 27(2): 585–608.

Cooter, R. (2000). Do good laws make good citizens? An economic analysis of internalized norms. *Virginia Law Review*, 86(8): 1577–601. Symposium: The Legal Construction of Norms.

Depoorter, B. and Vanneste, S. (2006). Norms and enforcement: The case against copyright litigation. *Oregon Law Review*, 84(4): 1127.

Dharmapala, D. (2006). The congressional budget process, aggregate spending, and statutory budget rules. *Journal of Public Economics*, 90: 119–41.

Dharmapala, D. and McAdams, R. H. (2003). The Condorcet jury theorem and the expressive function of law: A theory of informative law. *American Law and Economics Review*, 5(1): 1–31.

Dixit, A. K. and Pindyck, R. S. (1994). *Investment Under Uncertainty*. Princeton University Press, Princeton, NJ, USA.

Durkheim, E. (1965). *The Elementary Forms of Religious Life*. The Free Press, New York.

Ehrlich, I. and Posner, R. A. (1974). An economic analysis of legal rulemaking. *Journal of Legal Studies*, 3(1): 257–86.

Ellickson, R. C. (1991). *Order Without Law: How Neighbors Settle Disputes*. Harvard University Press, Cambridge, MA, USA.

Elster, J. (1991). *The Cement of Society*. Cambridge University Press, Cambridge, UK.

Epstein, R. (2011). Commenter, 13th Annual Faculty Conference of the Federalist Society, young scholars paper presentations, January 7.

Eskridge, W. N., Frickey, P. P., and Garrett, E. (2006). *Legislation and Statutory Interpretation*. Foundation Press, New York.

Feldman, Y. (2009). The expressive function of trade secret law: Legality, cost, intrinsic motivation, and consensus. *Journal of Empirical Legal Studies*, 6: 177–212.

Fon, V. and Parisi, F. (2008). Role-reversibility, stochastic ignorance, and social cooperation. *The Journal of Socio-Economics*, 37: 1061–75.

Foucault, M. (1990). *The History of Sexuality, Volume I: An Introduction*. Vintage Books, New York.

Fudenberg, D. and Harris, C. (1992). Evolutionary dynamics with aggregate shocks. *Journal of Economic Theory*, 57: 420–41.
Funk, P. (2007). Is there an expressive function of law? An empirical analysis of voting laws with symbolic fines. *American Law and Economics Review*, 9(1): 1–25.
Garrett, E. (1998). Harnessing politics: The dynamics of offset requirement in the tax legislative process. *The University of Chicago Law Review*, 65: 501.
Garrett, E. (2004). Comment: Accounting for the federal budget and its reform. *Harvard Journal on Legislation*, 41: 187.
Gersen, J. E. (2007). Temporary legislation. *University of Chicago Law Review*, 74: 247–98.
Gersen, J. E. and Posner, E. A. (2007). Timing rules and legal institutions. *Harvard Law Review*, 121: 543–89.
Granovetter, M. (1985). Economic action and social structure: The problem of embeddedness. *American Journal of Sociology*, 91: 481–510.
Grossman, G. M. and Helpman, E. (2001). *Special Interest Politics*. MIT Press, Cambridge, MA, USA and London.
Habermas, J. (1984). *The Theory of Communicative Action*. Beacon Press, Boston, MA, USA. Translated by Thomas McCarthy.
Harsanyi, J. C. and Selten, R. (1988). *A General Theory of Equilibrium Selection in Games*. MIT Press, Cambridge, MA, USA.
Hass, J. K. (2007). *Economic Sociology*. Routledge, New York.
Hassett, K. A. and Metcalf, G. E. (1999). Investment with uncertain tax policy: Does random tax policy discourage investment? *Economic Journal*, 109: 372.
Hume, D. ([1740] 1882). *Essays, Literary, Moral and Political*. Ward, Lock, London.
Kofford, K. J. and Miller, J. B. (2007). Habit, custom, and norms in economics. In Mercuro, N., editor, *Law and Economics: Critical Concepts in Law*, volume IV: *Social Norms and Law and Economics*, chapter 55, pages 21–36. Routledge, New York.
Kysar, R. M. (2006). The sun also rises: The political economy of sunset provisions in the tax code. *Georgia Law Review*, 40: 335.
Kysar, R. M. (2011). Lasting legislation. *University of Pennsylvania Law Review*, 159: 1007–68.
La Porta, R., de Silanes, F. L., and Shleifer, A. (2008). The economic consequences of legal origins. *Journal of Economic Literature*, 46: 285–332.

Landes, W. M. and Posner, R. A. (1975). The private enforcement of law. *Journal of Legal Studies*, 4: 1.

Landis, J. M. (1926). Constitutional limitations on the congressional power of investigation. *Harvard Law Review*, 40: 153.

Lewis, D. K. (1969). *Convention: A Philosophical Study*. Harvard University Press, Cambridge, MA, USA.

Lohmann, S. (1995). Information, access, and contributions: A signaling model of lobbying. *Public Choice*, 85: 267–84.

Luppi, B. and Parisi, F. (2009). Optimal timing of legal intervention: The role of timing rules. *Harvard Law Review Forum*, 122: 18–31.

Lyon, B. D. (1980). *A Constitutional and Legal History of Medieval England*. Norton, New York.

Marshall, A. (1961). *Principles of Economics, Volume I Text*. Macmillan, London, 9th (variorum) edition.

McAdams, R. H. (2000a). An attitudinal theory of expressive law. *University of Oregon Law Review*, 339.

McAdams, R. H. (2000b). A focal point theory of expressive law. *Virginia Law Review*, 86: 1649–729.

McAdams, R. H. and Rasmusen, E. B. (2005). *The Handbook of Law and Economics*, chapter, Norms in Law and Economics. Elsevier Science, Amsterdam.

McChesney, F. (1997). *Money for Nothing: Politicians, Rent Extraction, and Political Extortion*. Harvard University Press, Cambridge, MA, USA.

Messell, G. J. (1968). Law as an instrument of revolutionary change in a traditional milieu: The case of Soviet Central Asia. *Law and Society Review*, 2(2): 179–228.

Mill, J. S. (1872). *A System of Logic*. Longman, Green, Reader and Dyer, London, 8th edition.

Mitchell, L. E. (2007). Extracts from understanding norms. In Mercuro, N., editor, *Law and Economics: Critical Concepts in Law*, volume IV: *Social Norms and Law and Economics*, chapter 62, pages 225–79. Routledge, New York.

Nye, J. V. C. (2007). *War, Wine, and Taxes: The Political Economy of Anglo-French Trade, 1689–1900*. Princeton University Press, Princeton, NJ, USA.

Parisi, F., Fon, V., and Ghei, N. (2004). The value of waiting in lawmaking. *European Journal of Law and Economics*, 18: 131–48.

Posner, E. A. (2001). Controlling agencies with cost–benefit analysis:

A positive political theory perspective. *University of Chicago Law Review*, 68: 1137.

Posner, E. A. (2007). Introduction. In Parisi, F. and Posner, R. (series eds.), *Social Norms, Nonlegal Sanctions, and the Law*, volume 4 of *Economic Approaches to the Law*, pages ix–xv. Edward Elgar, Cheltenham, UK and Northampton, MA, USA.

Posner, E. A. and Vermeule, A. (2008). Crisis governance in the administrative state: 9/11 and the financial meltdown of 2008. John M. Olin Law & Economics Working Paper No. 440 (2nd Series).

Posner, R. A. (1983). *The Economics of Justice*. Harvard University Press, Cambridge, MA, USA.

Rasmusen, E. B. (1993). Lobbying when the decisionmaker can acquire independent information. *Public Choice*, 77: 899–913.

Samuelson, L. (1997). *Evolutionary Games and Equilibrium Selection*. MIT Press Series on Economic Learning and Social Evolution. MIT Press, Cambridge, MA, USA.

Samuelson, P. A. (1954). The pure theory of public expenditure. *The Review of Economics and Statistics*, 36: 387–9.

Stephenson, M. C. (2008). Evidentiary standards and information acquisition in public law. *American Law and Economics Review*, 10: 351–87.

Sunstein, C. R. (1996). Social norms and social roles. *Columbia Law Review*, 96: 903–68.

Sutinen, J. G. and Kuperan, K. (1999). A socio-economic theory of regulatory compliance. *International Journal of Social Economics*, 26: 174–93.

Traulsen, A., Claussen, J. C., and Hauert, C. (2005). Coevolutionary dynamics: From finite to infinite populations. *Physical Review Letters*, 95:238701.

Vermeule, A. (2009). *Law and the Limits of Reason*. Oxford University Press, New York.

Yin, G. K. (2009). Temporary-effect legislation, political accountability, and fiscal restraint. *New York University Law Review*, 84: 174.

Zasu, Y. (2008). Sanctions by social norms and the law: Substitutes or complements? *Journal of Legal Studies*, 36: 379–96.

Index